The Clockmaker's Apprentice

By: Mustafa Nejem

PROLOGUE

"The Clockmaker's Apprentice" Scarlett, an apprentice clockmaker, discovers that each clock possesses a unique rhythm corresponding to a moment in history. As she learns to adjust the clocks, she experiences these historical moments and gains insights into the fluidity of time.

CONTENTS

Chapter 1: The Meeting at the Store 4
Chapter 2: The Mysterious Book of Stories.. 7
Chapter 3: The First Adjustment.. 10
Chapter 4: Facing Temporal Dilemmas 13
Chapter 5: The Call of the Renaissance 15
Chapter 6: The Secret of the Master Clock.. 18
Chapter 7: Chaos in the French Revolution 21
Chapter 8: Alliances in the Future 24
Chapter 9: The Price of Knowledge... 26
Chapter 10: In Search of Atlantis... 29
Chapter 11: Journey into the Dark Abyss 32
Chapter 12: The Threat of the Paradox 35
Chapter 13: Awakening in the Middle Ages 37
Chapter 14: The Conclave of the Clocks 40
Chapter 15: Confrontation with an Ancestral Enemy 43
Chapter 16: The Revelation of the Master Clock 46
Chapter 17: Sacrifices for Balance... 49
Chapter 18: The Redemption of the Enemy... 51
Chapter 19: The Final Adjustment.. 53
Chapter 20: The New Beginning 56

Chapter 1

The Meeting
at the Store

Inside the shop, Scarlett is immersed in the task of repairing and restoring some of the watches that have lost their former glory. Every gear she adjusts and every spring she fixes seems to be an act of repair not only for the watches but also for the fragments of her own life still seeking harmony. Master Donovan, as he shares his ancestral knowledge, reveals the existence of a special clock, a hidden relic that might possess the power to alter the course of time. Conflict escalates when an enigmatic figure, a greedy collector seeking to seize the unique clock, enters the scene. This shadowy character unleashes a series of events that test Scarlett's loyalty to Master Donovan and the true nature of the bond between them. Emotions of betrayal and sacrifice intertwine, creating a tension reflected in the constant tick-tock of the surrounding clocks.

The cobblestone street and the shop become the epicenter of a confrontation that transcends the boundaries of time and space. Scarlett, propelled by the strength of her connection to the watches and to Master Donovan, embarks on a quest to preserve the integrity of time and protect the special clock from falling into the wrong hands. Every step she takes is a delicate dance between past and future, between the unraveling history and the one yet to be written. In the midst of this temporal whirlwind, Scarlett discovers not only the secrets of the watches but also the mysteries of her own identity and the deeper purpose that has led her to Master Donovan's shop. The narrative becomes a journey of self-discovery, where time is measured not only in hours and minutes but in revelations and transformations that transcend conventional logic. Master Donovan, the wise elder with a silver beard that waves like threads of time, observes Scarlett's entrance with eyes full of ancestral knowledge.

The wisdom emanating from him seems to be as ancient as the watches he keeps in his shop. The connection between Master Donovan and Scarlett goes beyond words; it is a resonance of souls united

by a shared fascination with time. In his gaze, there is a blend of curiosity and recognition, as if he had been waiting for someone like Scarlett to cross the threshold of his mysterious store. As their relationship deepens, crucial events are set in motion. Master Donovan shares stories that reveal not only the magic of the watches but also the emotional burden he carries. Scarlett, in turn, uncovers hidden secrets in each gear, weaving a closer bond with the elder. The watches she restores become bridges to the past, where prominent emotions such as lost love and redemption intertwine with the constant tick-tock of the clocks. The key conflict arises when a greedy collector jeopardizes the harmony of the shop, threatening to destroy the delicate balance of time.

Master Donovan and Scarlett are compelled to confront danger, unleashing intense emotions of courage and sacrifice. In this temporal dance, the shop becomes the stage for a battle between opposing forces, where each tick-tock resonates with the

struggle between good and evil. Initially, Scarlett immerses herself in the shop's daily routines, dedicating herself to meticulous tasks that connect her with the very essence of the watches. Her devotion to details goes beyond cleaning the accumulated dust on the watches and organizing tools; each action is a ritual that brings her closer to the magic contained within these timekeeping artifacts. Master Donovan, observing her dedication, begins to entrust deeper secrets of the shop to her, revealing the story behind each watch and the importance of her role in the temporal chain. As Scarlett delves into the world of watches, her connection with the constant tick-tock intensifies.

The sound seems to take on a life of its own, whispers from the past intertwining with the present. Prominent emotions like fascination and intrigue meld with the rhythmic pulsation of the watches, transforming the shop into a sanctuary where time comes to life. Crucial events unfold when Scarlett discovers a particularly ancient watch that, upon repair, unveils fragments of a forgotten story that unexpectedly connects her to her own lineage. The tick-tock then becomes a guiding thread that weaves the past and the present, creating an invisible bond between Scarlett and the unchanging flow of time. One day, driven by her insatiable curiosity, Scarlett decides to venture into the hidden workshop behind the shop, a space that had remained veiled in mystery until now. As she pushes the door, the creaking reveals the entrance to a forgotten corner, where unused watches rest on dust-covered shelves, like silent witnesses of times gone by.

Amongst the shadows and the scent of antiquity, Scarlett discovers the darkest and dustiest corner, where the special clock, Master Donovan's forgotten treasure, seems to glow faintly. The moment her eyes fall upon this lost gem becomes a crucial event. The clock emits a dim light resonating with an aura of ancient wisdom, as if patiently awaiting the right moment to be uncovered. The connection between Scarlett and the special clock intensifies, unleashing prominent emotions of awe and admiration. However, this revelation also triggers a key conflict, as the existence of the special clock attracts the attention of external forces seeking to seize its power. In this forgotten corner, Scarlett finds herself at the epicenter of a story that transcends time, where the flickering light of the special clock promises to unveil secrets that will alter the course of her own life. When Scarlett holds the special clock in her hands, a magical resonance seems to flow between her and the ancient artifact.

A strange connection is established, as if the pulses of the clock were an echo of her own heart, and the tick-tocks become an ancestral melody whispering secrets buried in the fabric of time. Each swing of the pendulum seems to narrate a lost story to Scarlett, as if the clock were a guardian of forgotten narratives. The fascination in Scarlett's eyes does not go unnoticed by Master Donovan, who, sensing the intensity of the connection, decides that the time has come to share with her the deepest secrets

of horology. His wise smile reveals an understanding beyond words, a connection between master and apprentice that transcends the complexities of watches.

In this pivotal moment, the master decides to open the doors of wisdom, unleashing a cascade of events that will reveal not only the mysteries of the special clock but also the ties that bind Scarlett to a destiny that transcends the hands of time.

Master Donovan, recognizing the special connection between Scarlett and the clock, entrusts her with the crucial task of restoring the mysterious artifact as a fundamental part of her training. The responsibility weighs on Scarlett's shoulders, but her determination is fueled by the opportunity to unravel the secrets locked within the heart of time. As she disassembles each piece of the clock, reality transforms into a sort of journey through time. She discovers that the gears and springs carry the very essence of key moments in history, as if each component were a silent witness to the events that have shaped the course of happenings. Every screw Scarlett removes reveals a small door to the past, and through this opening, she immerses herself in scenes trapped in the folds of time. Prominent emotions of nostalgia and discovery envelop her as she reconstructs the clock, feeling that each action is a way to rescue forgotten fragments of history.

This restoration process not only becomes a test of skill but also an emotional journey where Scarlett discovers that her connection to the clock goes beyond mere mechanics; it is a gateway to a deeper understanding of herself and the threads that weave the fabric of time. During the repair, the special clock suddenly activates, enveloping Scarlett in a blinding light. Suddenly, she finds herself in the bustling Industrial Revolution, surrounded by smoking factories and workers fighting for their rights. The excitement and turmoil of that era completely immerse her. Back in the shop, Scarlett realizes that she has unearthed something extraordinary. The special clock not only marks time; it is a portal to history.

This first time travel experience awakens in Scarlett an insatiable desire to understand the connection between watches and historical moments.

Master Donovan, seeing the spark in his apprentice's eyes, knows that this is just the first stop on a journey that will change their lives and the very understanding of reality. The shop becomes the starting point of a temporal odyssey, where each tick-tock reveals hidden secrets in the gears of the past.

Chapter 2

The Mysterious
Book of Stories

After her journey to the Industrial Revolution, Scarlett returns to the shop eager to uncover more secrets of time. The experience in the past has left an indelible mark on her being, and her eyes reflect a mix of astonishment and determination. Master Donovan, attuned to the excitement in his apprentice, decides to take her to a hidden corner of the shop, where ancient scrolls and manuscripts fill dusty shelves. Each scroll seems like an echo from bygone eras, and Scarlett feels that ancestral knowledge permeates the air around her. She finds a leather-bound book, whose pages seem to pulsate with the very essence of time. Scarlett's hands tremble slightly as she opens it, and as her eyes traverse the pages, she delves into narratives that surpass her understanding. Prominent emotions of astonishment and reverence envelop her as she discovers the intricacies of the relationship between watches and history.

This discovery not only triggers an internal conflict in Scarlett, who struggles to assimilate the vastness of the information, but also propels her to confront new challenges and discoveries that will expand her understanding of time and her own role in this intertwined fabric of past, present, and future. Intrigued, Scarlett opens the leather-bound book and immerses herself in its pages, as if she were opening a door to a vast realm of knowledge. She discovers detailed accounts of watches that have been witnesses and participants in crucial moments of history. Each story, meticulously recorded on the yellowed pages, reveals the magical connection that watches maintain with events of the past, like threads weaving the tapestry of time. She becomes immersed in narratives where watches have set the cadence of epic battles, been accomplices to forbidden loves, and recorded the pulse of social revolutions. Scarlett's emotions overflow as she assimilates the depth of watches' influence on human history.

Awe and reverence envelop her, as each story is a tangible reminder of the significance of her work in Master Donovan's shop. As she progresses through the pages, she feels intertwined with the characters and events, as if the book itself is guiding her through a journey across time. This discovery not only expands her understanding of the role of watches but also deepens her connection with the very fabric of time, marking a turning point in her journey of self-discovery and revealing the weight of responsibility resting on her shoulders.

Among the detailed stories in the book, Scarlett finds a particularly captivating account of a watch that marked the exact moment when a crucial peace treaty was signed between two conflicting nations. Each word is a thread weaving the narrative of that historic moment, and Scarlett immerses herself in the story with intense attention.

As she absorbs the words, she feels a strange connection to that specific moment in history, as if she were present at the time and place where the treaty was sealed. The magic of the narrative envelops her, and for a moment, the past and the present intertwine surprisingly. Intense emotions, such as the solemnity of the treaty and the hope it brought, flow through Scarlett. The connection with the watch becomes a visceral experience, as if she had touched a tangible fragment of the past. This discovery not only adds another layer of complexity to her relationship with watches but also awakens a profound understanding of the responsibility that comes with working with artifacts that have witnessed momentous events in human history.

With each page Scarlett turns, the young watchmaker is immersed in internal conflicts. The responsibility to safeguard these historical secrets clashes with the temptation to intervene and alter the course of history to prevent tragedies.

Master Donovan, sensing Scarlett's struggle, warns her about the fragility of the temporal fabric and the importance of respecting the natural order of events. Scarlett wrestles between her desire to change fate and the wisdom that urges her to be a responsible guardian of time. Every word whispers not only stories of the past but also the profound implications of her role in the inexorable flow of time.

Scarlett's connection to the past intensifies with each page read, creating a whirlwind of emotions. Each story imbues her being with the richness of historical events, and the temptation to alter the course of events becomes a seductive call. However, this desire is tempered by the fear of unforeseen consequences that could be unleashed by interfering with time. Scarlett is plunged into internal conflicts, torn between the longing to be a figure shaping destiny and the awareness that the temporal fabric is fragile and complex.

Master Donovan, sensing his apprentice's struggle, becomes a guide and advisor, warning her about the ramifications of her choices. The emotional tension intensifies, marking a crucial point in Scarlett's journey, where she must balance her fascination with the past with the responsibility to preserve the integrity of time. As Scarlett delves deeper into the mysterious book, she begins to notice clues and recurring mentions of an intriguing enigma: the "Master Clock." This clock, which appears to be the key to all others, becomes the central focus of her quest. Each page is a clue, and every story about watches takes her one step closer to unraveling the mystery that seems to govern the destinies of the artifacts and time itself.

Scarlett's fascination with this enigma blends with a growing determination. The book, now her guide, leads her through the eras in a temporal odyssey, exploring crucial moments where the "Master Clock" has left its mark.

The conflict intensifies as Scarlett discovers that the truth behind the "Master Clock" may have monumental consequences. The temptation to unveil the enigma clashes with Master Donovan's warning about the fragility of time. Emotions of intrigue and anxiety intertwine as Scarlett embarks on a journey that not only takes her through epochs and places but also towards an understanding of her own role in this temporal fabric. The quest for the "Master Clock" not only becomes a key conflict but also a journey that challenges the barriers of time and Scarlett's wisdom about what it means to be a guardian of watches and history itself. Scarlett, determined and passionate, dives into the search for the "Master Clock," ready to face whatever challenges it may present. Her emotions fluctuate between the fascination with the knowledge she is gaining and the unease about the responsibility it carries. Each page of the mysterious book is a blank leaf in her own temporal odyssey. The shop, with its silent watches and the key artifact that guides her, becomes the epicenter of an adventure that will lead her to unravel the deepest secrets of temporality. In this journey, Scarlett will not only confront the mysteries of the past but also the internal challenges posed by the weight of her new mission.

Chapter 3

The First
Adjustment

Scarlett, infused with the knowledge from the mysterious book, stands before the worktable in Master Donovan's shop. The ancient clock, a silent witness to the Industrial Revolution, patiently awaits her trembling yet determined hands. Each tick-tock of the artifact resonates with the history it carries, and Scarlett feels the weight of responsibility for the task entrusted to her. Master Donovan, with wise eyes and serene confidence, assigns her the task of making her first adjustment to this historically significant artifact. In this pivotal moment, Scarlett faces the duality of emotions: fascination for the clock and concern about the possibility of altering its delicate balance. The shop, filled with whispers from the past, becomes the stage where the next chapter of her temporal adventure will unfold, as Scarlett, guided by Master

Donovan's wisdom, sets out to unravel the deepest secrets of history that await in the shadows of time.

With a mixture of nervousness and determination, Scarlett immerses herself in the task of disassembling the ancient clock. Each piece she removes reveals the history engraved in its mechanism, like chapters of an ancient book. The constant tick-tock resonates like the pulse of a bygone era, enveloping her in the essence of moments the clock has witnessed. As she adjusts the delicate pieces, Scarlett feels a unique connection with time, as if she is weaving her destiny with every turn of the key. Emotions oscillate between reverence for the unfolding history before her and the anxiety of being the guardian of this temporal fragment. The shop becomes a sanctuary where past and present converge, and Scarlett, amid whispers of time, advances in the delicate dance of adjusting the gears, feeling that each movement shapes not only the clock but also her own role in the weaving of time. The light flickers, and suddenly, Scarlett finds herself immersed in the Industrial Revolution.

The bustling factory greets her with deafening noise and thick smoke hanging in the air. Adorned in period clothing, Scarlett becomes a firsthand witness to the harsh reality of the workers and the working conditions. The tension in the air is palpable, and the struggle for the rights of those whose lives are intertwined with the constant movement of machines resonates in every corner. Scarlett's emotions intertwine with the surroundings, feeling the fatigue in the bodies of the workers and the determination in their gazes. The oppressive atmosphere of the place seeps through time, and Scarlett, imbued by the experience, adjusts the clock with a mix of respect and sympathy for those who suffered in the Industrial Revolution.

The shop becomes a temporal bridge where empathy merges with the mechanics of time, and Scarlett, upon returning to her present, carries the indelible traces of an experience that transcends the gears of the clock.

In this historical setting, Scarlett encounters key figures of the Industrial Revolution. From visionary inventors to brave labor leaders, each encounter reveals the complexity of their lives and the challenges they face in their quest for meaningful change. Scarlett becomes entangled in the plot of history, participating in clandestine conversations and witnessing crucial moments that existed only in history books.

The figure of a passionate inventor, whose dreams are intertwined with the machinery Scarlett is adjusting, unveils the hope and sacrifice that innovation entails. In conversations with labor leaders, she experiences the strength and desperation of those fighting for fair working conditions. Master Donovan's shop becomes a sanctuary where the past comes to life, and Scarlett, with a deeper understanding of humanity, adjusts the clock with hands that now bear the weight of the stories she has lived.

As Scarlett returns to her time, her emotions are a blend of awe and respect, feeling the influence of the past in every fiber of her being.

The experience not only transforms her as a clockmaker but also as a guardian of the silent testimonies that watches carry with them. The shop, once a refuge, becomes a sanctuary of stories woven into the very fabric of time. However, the act of adjusting the clock becomes an ethical dilemma.

Scarlett, immersed in the Industrial Revolution, realizes that her actions have the power to directly influence the events she witnesses.

The temptation to intervene to help those who are suffering clashes with Master Donovan's resonant warning in her mind: the delicate balance of time must not be disturbed. Every turn of the key and every gear adjustment becomes decisions weighing on Scarlett's shoulders.

The struggle to stay true to her ethics is reflected in her gestures as she wrestles between the desire to change the fate of those she meets in the past and the respect for the integrity of the temporal fabric. The shop, once a haven of learning, becomes the stage for an internal conflict where emotions intertwine with crucial decisions that will determine not only the fate of the watches but also the

impact Scarlett will have on history itself. Scarlett's internal conflict reaches its climax as she grapples between intervention and historical preservation. The responsibility not to alter the temporal fabric clashes with the passionate desire to change the destiny of those whose lives are marked by the wheels of the Industrial Revolution. Each adjustment of the clock becomes a dilemma, and emotions collide like conflicting gears. Scarlett, with trembling hands, becomes the bridge between two worlds, dealing with the potential consequences of each choice.

The shop, becomes filled with palpable tension as Scarlett navigates the fine line between positive influence and respect for temporal integrity. In this crucial moment, the young clockmaker confronts not only the secrets of the watches but also the immutable truth of her own ability to shape the course of history. Scarlett returns to the shop with the modified clock. Master Donovan, observing her return, understands the journey she has undergone. The clock now bears the imprint of her intervention, a scar in time. The young clockmaker faces Master Donovan with a mixture of triumph and fear, aware that her act has left a permanent mark on history. The elderly master, with wise eyes, senses the emotional burden Scarlett carries. As he contemplates the altered clock, the shop is filled with a silent tension, as if time itself is weighing the decisions of its guardian.

Scarlett reflects on the consequences of her first adjustment and the deeper burden of her connection with time, feeling that each resonant tick-tock in the shop is an echo of the decisions she has made and the responsibilities that now weigh on her shoulders. The shop, with its motionless clocks and the echo of the Industrial Revolution in its memory, becomes a sanctuary that treasures the lessons learned. The delicate dance between the present and the past persists, and Scarlett delves even further into the temporal odyssey that will change her in ways she cannot fully comprehend yet.

Chapter 4

Facing
Temporal Dilemmas

Scarlett, with the echo of time travels resonating in her mind, delves deeper into her role as the custodian of time in Master Donovan's shop. Each adjustment to the special clocks takes her through a tapestry of historical moments, from the Renaissance to the space age. Each journey, however, brings with it ethical dilemmas that challenge the very essence of her duty as a temporal horologist. Scarlett, amid the shadows of the past and the whispers of the future, faces the ongoing struggle to reconcile her passion for history with the responsibility of being the guardian of its integrity.

In the Renaissance, Scarlett finds herself surrounded by the creative effervescence and intellectual flourishing. She interacts with visionary artists and innovative scientists, absorbing the cultural richness of the era.

Master Donovan's shop becomes a portal to the halls of great minds, where each adjustment to the special clocks is also a step through the pages of history. However, when faced with the possibility of preventing a historical tragedy, Scarlett's internal struggle intensifies. The temptation to change destiny clashes against Maestro Donovan's stern warning about the unpredictable consequences of altering the course of time. In this ethical conflict, Scarlett becomes entangled in the momentous decisions that mark not only history but also her own sense of responsibility as the guardian of time. Each era she travels to poses a moral challenge. From the French Revolution to the Industrial Revolution, Scarlett confronts difficult decisions. The whispers of the clocks blend with her own sighs as she tries to balance her love for history with the duty to preserve temporal integrity.

The shop, witnessing these tensions, becomes a crucible of emotions where the past and the future converge, and Scarlett, amidst the weight of her choices and the constant fascination with time, continues her journey, weaving the tapestry of history with each tick-tock. In World War II, Scarlett

immerses herself in the devastation and courage of those dark times. Master Donovan's shop becomes a portal to a period marked by heroism and sacrifice. Scarlett experiences moments of intensity, where humanity confronts its worst instincts and its noblest gestures.

As she interacts with characters who have left an indelible mark on history, from brave soldiers to resilient civilians, her understanding of human complexity deepens. However, the temptation to influence the outcome of the war also looms over her. The line between good and evil blurs, and Scarlett finds herself in an overwhelming ethical dilemma.

The burden of knowing the future clashes with the responsibility to respect the integrity of time. Each adjustment to the clocks becomes a crucial choice. In the dimness of the shop, Scarlett wrestles between the need to preserve history as it is and the temptation to alter events to prevent tragedies.

The whispers of the clocks seem to intensify, as if the past itself were engaging in a dialogue with her. The shop is filled with the palpable tension of a period marked by human duality, where hope coexists with despair, and Scarlett, amidst the tangle of ethical decisions, becomes the weaver of a destiny entwined with the immutable flow of time. In this journey, she not only witnesses historical events but also the complexity that defines them, carrying the emotional scars of a past that resists being forgotten. Back in the shop, Scarlett faces the silent judgment of the clocks, mute witnesses to her choices and decisions.

Master Donovan, with his accumulated wisdom spanning centuries, guides Scarlett, he reminds her of the importance of respecting the temporal structure and the unpredictable ramifications of intervening in crucial events. The ancient clocks, with their dials marked by history, seem to watch her with invisible eyes as Scarlett reflects on her role as a custodian of time. Each tick-tock resonates as a constant reminder of the fragility of temporal balance. In that sanctuary of ancestral timepieces, Scarlett encounters characters whose destinies are intertwined with the currents of time: from visionary artists and scientists to anonymous soldiers who forged their legacy in the pages of history. Master Donovan, with silver beard and eyes full of knowledge, becomes Scarlett's beacon, guiding her through the tumultuous tides of time. The lessons he imparts go beyond the mechanics of clocks; they are lessons about responsibility, humility, and understanding that the flow of time is a delicate balance between intervention and preservation.

In her travels, Scarlett experiences the darkest moments of humanity and its brightest epochs. From devastating wars to cultural rebirths, the young watchmaker undergoes the complexity of time and the consequences of her actions. The shop becomes a sanctuary where the past converges with the present, and Scarlett, amidst whispers of forgotten chronologies, faces not only decisions but also the consequences of being the weaver of history. The shop, with its motionless clocks and the murmurs of temporal consequences, becomes a haven for reflection. Scarlett, more aware than ever of the

fragility of time, is immersed in the silence surrounding the clocks, each one telling its own story. Master Donovan, with his wise and serene presence, becomes the guide leading her to the next chapter of her temporal odyssey. The young watchmaker, with eyes filled with the weight of past decisions, embarks on the next phase of her unique journey through history.

The clocks, as silent witnesses, seem to accompany her on her journey, whispers of past times resonating in every corner of the shop. Scarlett, ready to unravel more mysteries and face even deeper dilemmas, immerses herself in the constant flow of time, carrying with her the lessons learned and the determination to weave her own destiny into the eternal tapestry of history.

Chapter 5

The Call of
the Renaissance

Scarlett, imbued with responsibility and excitement, immerses herself in the task of adjusting the clock that will connect her directly to the Renaissance. Every turn of the key and every precise adjustment bring her closer to an era of overflowing creativity and revolutionary discoveries. The clocks, on their silent shelves, seem to throb with the expectation of events to come. Scarlett, with skillful hands and a fearless heart, becomes the weaver of her own temporal destiny, ready to unravel the mysteries and wonders that the Renaissance holds for her. While making the adjustments, Scarlett experiences the unique vibration that indicates the opening of the temporal portal to the Renaissance. The light flickers, and suddenly, she finds herself immersed in a Renaissance city, surrounded by art that has endured through the centuries.

The cobblestone streets overflow with life, with street artists displaying their skills and lively markets filled with vibrant colors. The majestic architecture of the era stands before her, a witness to an age of cultural flourishing. Scarlett, with eyes illuminated by wonder, explores this world of unrestrained creativity. She encounters Leonardo da Vinci immersed in his masterpieces and crosses paths with Michelangelo, whose sculptures seem to come to life. Master Donovan's shop, now a timeless beacon in the heart of the Renaissance, harmoniously blends with the artistic richness that surrounds her. However, amid the exuberance of the Renaissance, ethical dilemmas arise for Scarlett. She faces the temptation to intervene and alter the course of history, perhaps influencing the creation of masterpieces or protecting iconic figures of the time. Responsibility clashes with fascination, and Scarlett, though captivated by the greatness of the era, strives to remember Master Donovan's lessons about the delicate balance of time.

As she adjusts the clock to return to her own time, Scarlett carries with her the essence of the Renaissance, where each tick-tock seems to resonate with the inspiration and ingenuity of that golden period. Back in the shop, Master Donovan welcomes her with a wise smile, acknowledging the growth of his apprentice in this unique temporal journey. Adorned in garments of the era, Scarlett blends into the rich cultural tapestry of the Renaissance. Her attire harmonizes with the elegance of the time, and every step on the cobblestone streets is like a journey through a living canvas. She interacts with masters like Leonardo da Vinci and Michelangelo, witnesses to their creative genius and the complexities of the artistic process. Emotions flow as Scarlett engages in dialogues with brilliant minds like Galileo and Copernicus, who share their revolutionary vision of the cosmos. The vibrant atmosphere of artistic and scientific discussions envelops her, plunging her into a sea of innovative ideas.

In every corner of the Renaissance, the creations that have endured in history and whose influence reaches into the present unfold. The temptation to intervene and guide these geniuses in their pursuit of knowledge becomes increasingly stronger. The responsibility not to alter the natural flow of time clashes with the fascination of being part of crucial moments in history.

In her interactions with the great masters, Scarlett discovers not only the genius that defines them but also the humanity they share. The pressures of creation, doubts, and the relentless pursuit of truth are revealed in intimate conversations. As Scarlett experiences the vastness of the Renaissance, the complexity of emotions becomes the thread that guides her temporal journey, woven into every corner of this golden era. However, the beauty of the Renaissance also unveils conflicts and dilemmas inherent to the time.

The powerful influence of the Church, the tensions between science and deeply rooted traditions, all place Scarlett in the midst of heated debates. The young watchmaker, adorned in the attire of the time and grappling with cultural complexities, finds herself immersed in a world where the duality between reason and faith sets the pulse of Renaissance society. Conversations with the masters introduce her to the internal struggles of those times, where innovative ideas clashed with the restrictions imposed by existing structures.

Scarlett, aware of the delicate temporal dance, strives not to alter the crucial events that will shape the course of history, while her heart is caught in the dilemma of balancing the preservation of temporal integrity and the temptation to influence the unfolding of ideas and creations that will leave an indelible mark on humanity. Scarlett is faced with the opportunity to prevent a historically significant tragedy.

Although the desire to alleviate human suffering is strong, the responsibility to preserve the integrity of time stands in her way. Scarlett's internal struggle manifests in a series of difficult decisions, each carrying emotional weight and ethical burdens. Choices present themselves as crossroads, where each divergent path could change the course of history. Tormented by the knowledge of unforeseeable consequences, Scarlett is immersed in an internal battle between the duty not to alter the natural flow of time and the urgency to intervene to prevent tragedies. Amidst this conflict, the young watchmaker

discovers the complexity of the human condition, where joy and sorrow, creation and destruction, are intertwined in the fabric of time. Every decision she makes resonates with the emotions and dilemmas inherent in the unique position she holds as a guardian of the temporal fabric. Back in the shop, Scarlett encounters the wise gaze of Master Donovan.

Without judgment, he guides her through the complexities of her choices. The watch, now adjusted and marked by Scarlett's experiences in the Renaissance, becomes a testament to the difficult decisions the young watchmaker has faced. Each tick-tock seems to carry the echo of moral crossroads and conflicting emotions woven into the fabric of time. Master Donovan, with his millennia-old knowledge, understands the unique burden Scarlett carries on her shoulders. In his gaze, there is a mix of admiration for her courage and the wisdom of one who understands the inherent complexities of being a custodian of time. The shop, in silence, witnesses Scarlett's development, becoming the silent witness to the choices that have shaped her connection with history and the crucial role she plays in preserving temporal integrity. Scarlett returns to the shop, reflecting on the lessons learned and the ongoing responsibility that her connection with time entails.

The shop, with its watches that have witnessed complete eras, becomes a silent witness to the temporal drama unfolding through the eyes and hands of the young watchmaker. With each adjustment, Scarlett delves deeper into the complexity of her role as the guardian of temporal secrets, preparing to face new eras and challenges in her odyssey through time.. Far from just an apprentice, Scarlett has become the weaver of temporal stories, a being that moves between the lines of time with a defined purpose.

Chapter 6

The Secret of
the Master Clock

Scarlett, after her experience in the Renaissance, returns to the shop with a deeper understanding of her role as a temporal guardian. The maturity she has gained does not go unnoticed by Master Donovan, who, in a dark and enigmatic corner of the shop, decides to share with her the best-kept secret: the existence of the "Master Clock." In that corner, surrounded by ancient watches and worn scrolls, Master Donovan reveals to Scarlett the truth behind this mystical artifact that seems to be the key to all others. The "Master Clock" is not only an instrument that controls the flow of time but also the connection between individual watches and their shared temporal fabric. Scarlett's gaze lights up with a mix of astonishment and understanding as Master Donovan invites her to unravel the mysteries of this unique clock that will guide her next phase in the odyssey through the eras.

Master Donovan, knowing that Scarlett is ready to face new challenges, reveals to her the legend of the Master Clock, an artifact that supposedly controls all other temporal watches. In a secluded corner of the shop, amidst shadows and the gentle ticking of watches, Master Donovan shares with Scarlett the story of this mythical artifact. According to legend, the Master Clock not only controls the flow of time but is also intertwined with the fate of those who guard temporal continuity. Scarlett, feeling a mix of astonishment and determination, decides to embark on the quest for this mysterious clock to understand the true nature of time and her role as a temporal guardian.

The shop, with its atmosphere laden with temporal secrets, becomes the starting point for a new and fascinating stage in Scarlett's odyssey through the eras. The path to the Master Clock leads Scarlett through multiple epochs and challenges.

Master Donovan, with his silver beard wafting in the breeze of time, hands her fragments encoded in ancient manuscripts and artifacts, guiding her on a quest that spans centuries of history. Each adjustment of the clock becomes a dimensional door that transports Scarlett to different eras, from the splendor of the Renaissance to the darkness of World War II. At every step, she discovers more about temporal complexity and faces obstacles planted by unknown forces attempting to thwart her mission. The Master Clock becomes an enigma connecting the ages and challenges Scarlett to understand not only time but also her own role in weaving destiny. As the young clockmaker advances, Master Donovan's shop becomes a haven between eras, a point of stability amid the temporal whirlwind that envelops her. Mysterious characters emerge

from the shadows of time, and tumultuous events stand in her way, revealing the existence of a resistance seeking to keep the Master Clock hidden. The young clockmaker becomes entangled in ethical dilemmas as she progresses toward the core of the temporal secret. In each era, she uncovers fragments of encoded information pointing to the location of the mythical artifact. However, the temporal resistance, with its own motives and agendas, seeks to stop her, sowing distrust and challenges in her path. Master Donovan's shop becomes a bastion of knowledge and temporal refuge, where Scarlett prepares to face the unexpected twists of her journey to the Master Clock.

The mixture of intrigue and determination in her eyes reflects the growing understanding that her quest will not only impact the course of time but also unveil universal truths that have remained hidden for eons. Each clock adjustment provides Scarlett glimpses of the true power of the Master Clock. She discovers the intricate connection between this artifact and the fates of key individuals in history.

With each turn of the key and delicate adjustment, Scarlett delves deeper into the intricacies of the temporal fabric. As she unravels the hidden secrets behind the Master Clock, she also grapples with the burden of understanding the responsibilities that come with her knowledge. The duality of fascination and fear envelops her as she realizes that her quest is not just an exploration of temporal mysteries but also a confrontation with the consequences of possessing such knowledge in a world where temporal balance is fragile and susceptible to the decisions of those who guard it. The temptation to manipulate events for a greater good clashes with Master Donovan's warning about the unpredictable consequences of playing with such powerful temporal forces. Scarlett stands at an ethical crossroads, facing decisions that could alter the very essence of reality. Each encounter with the Master Clock reveals deeper layers of her connection to time and the responsibility that rests upon her shoulders.

The tension mounts as Scarlett delves into the pages of the past, unraveling secrets that could change the course of history. However, the shadow of unknown consequences haunts her, creating an

emotional dilemma that torments her with every tick-tock of the clock. The quest for the Master Clock becomes a journey not only through time but also into Scarlett's own morality, challenging her limits and forcing her to confront the true nature of her role as the guardian of time. Scarlett approaches the place where the Master Clock is believed to reside. The store, with its collection of silent watches, becomes the epicenter of the search. Scarlett, with determination and fear, prepares to unravel the secret that could change not only her understanding of time but the very structure of temporal existence. Scarlett's odyssey ventures into even more mysterious territories, facing the possibility of astonishing discoveries.

Each step takes her beyond familiar limits, where time seems to acquire new dimensions, and the watches, silent witnesses, anticipate the transcendental revelation. The tension in the air is palpable as Scarlett confronts the enigma, joining forces with the very fabric of time. With each swing of the pendulum, the young watchmaker plunges into the final phase of her quest, feeling the weight of responsibility and the excitement of uncovering the truth that lies behind the Master Clock.

Chapter 7

Chaos in the
French Revolution

Scarlett, immersed in the fervor of the French Revolution, receives the task of adjusting a clock linked to this tumultuous period. The responsibility of intervening in such a crucial moment in history weighs on her shoulders as Maestro Donovan warns her about the unpredictable ramifications of her actions. Scarlett finds herself transported to the bustling streets of Paris, where the struggle for freedom and equality unfolds before her eyes. Witness to events that would shape the course of a nation, Scarlett faces the duality of her role as a watchmaker and guardian of time. The revolutionary passion and the voices of the oppressed resonate in her ears as she, with trembling hands, makes the adjustments that could alter the course of the Revolution. Scarlett finds herself entangled in the web of history, where each tick-tock of the clock seems to weave her destiny with the very fate of the French Revolution.

In the streets of Paris, Scarlett finds herself amidst revolutionary turmoil. The cries for equality and freedom resonate in the air, and the young watchmaker dons period attire to immerse herself in the whirlwind of the French Revolution. The guillotine stands as a symbol of the quest for justice and the fall of the aristocracy. As Scarlett adjusts the clock linked to this tumultuous period, she experiences the tension and fervor of street protests. Historical figures, with their ideals and conflicts, come to life around her. Scarlett is caught in the duality of her duty and the temptation to alter events to alleviate the suffering of those whose fates are intertwined with the Revolution. Each adjustment becomes a delicate act, where the pulse of history beats in every tick-tock of the clock.

The young watchmaker grapples with preserving temporal integrity and the urgency to influence a critical moment that will change the course of humanity.

While adjusting the clock linked to this period, Scarlett encounters key figures of the Revolution. Robespierre, Danton, and Marat, passionate leaders with divergent visions, envelop her in intense debates about the limits of freedom and equality. Scarlett, caught in the whirlwind of ideologies, faces the moral complexity of her own actions. The guillotine, a silent witness to the quest for justice,

becomes a tangible reminder of the deadly consequences of the revolt. The young watchmaker immerses herself in the lives of ordinary citizens, feeling the burden of suffering and hope with each clock adjustment. Crucial moments of the French Revolution unfold before her, and the temptation to change the course of history to alleviate the weight of oppression blends with Maestro Donovan's persistent warning about the fragility of the temporal fabric. Amidst turmoil and ethical dilemmas, Scarlett seeks to balance her duty as a guardian of time with the compassion she feels for those trapped in the gears of the Revolution.

As she becomes more involved in the French Revolution, the temptation to alter the course of crucial events is presented to her. The opportunity to mitigate suffering and guide the Revolution down a less bloody

path contrasts with Maestro Donovan's warning about the unpredictable consequences of her interventions in the timeline. Scarlett, feeling the intensity of revolutionary ideals and the burden of injustice, is caught in an ethical dilemma. Her heart leans towards compassion for the oppressed, but the wisdom of the Master resonates in her mind, reminding her of the fragility of temporal balance. While adjusting the clock linked to this tumultuous period, voices from the past whisper moral dilemmas to her, and Scarlett faces the decision to be a mere observer or an active influence in the French Revolution. Each tick-tock of the clock seems to echo the choices that will resonate in history, and the young watchmaker finds herself at the epicenter of a crossroads,

Scarlett finds herself caught between her duty as a guardian of time and the passionate desire to assist those who struggle for freedom. Every choice she makes, every word she utters, could have unforeseen repercussions in the French Revolution and, consequently, in the entire fabric of time. Amidst heated discussions and growing tensions, Scarlett experiences a whirlwind of emotions. The cruelty of the guillotine and the cries of the crowd confront her with the harsh reality of the Revolution. Her internal conflict reaches its peak when she faces the crossroads of intervening to change the fate of those fighting for freedom or maintaining the integrity of the temporal fabric.

During critical moments such as the Storming of the Bastille and the trial of Louis XVI, Scarlett, between history and her own emotions, navigates through a sea of chaos where every decision weighs heavily. The ethical tension reaches its climax as she confronts moral dilemmas that could alter the destiny of nations.

The crowd demands justice, and Scarlett, burdened by her temporal knowledge, finds herself at the epicenter of a revolt that could alter the course of French history.

Desperation and hope intertwine as she struggles to balance her duty as a guardian of time and her desire to alleviate human suffering. In this whirlwind of events, Scarlett faces not only the challenges of the French Revolution but also the uncomfortable truth that her actions have consequences beyond her initial understanding. Back in the shop, Maestro Donovan, with a wise gaze, observes Scarlett's return. The clock, now adjusted, bears the mark of the young clockmaker's decisions in the French Revolution. Scarlett reflects on the lessons learned and the inevitable consequences of her actions,

while the shop, with its silent clocks, guards the secrets of a tumultuous era in human history. The experience in the French Revolution has left traces on Scarlett's soul.

The echo of the guillotine and the cries for justice resonates in her mind as she immerses herself in the task of adjusting the next clock. Ethical tension persists, as each of her actions could have unimaginable consequences. Master Donovan, as a guide through the twists of time, encourages her to learn from each experience, even when moral dilemmas push her to the limit. The clocks in the shop, with their silent and steady march, seem to whisper the complexity of time. Scarlett, feeling the burden of her role, prepares for the next phase of her temporal odyssey. The connection between past, present, and future is revealed as an intricate fabric, and Scarlett, as the weaver of that destiny, is poised to face new challenges and discoveries in her unique journey through time. The shop, with its timeless atmosphere, becomes the refuge where Scarlett finds the balance between fascination for knowledge and the responsibility that comes with her role as a guardian of time.

Chapter 8

Alliances in the Future

Scarlett, determined to unravel the mysteries of the Master Clock, embarks on a new phase of her temporal odyssey. Master Donovan, sensing the magnitude of the quest, guides the young clockmaker toward forming alliances with other apprentices who have discovered the power of clocks. Together, they explore the symphony of time, merging knowledge and experiences from different eras. The once-silent shop now resonates with the collaboration of curious minds and skilled hands. The group, a temporal crucible, faces challenges and revelations that will take them beyond the limits of the past and the future. In a special corner of the shop, Scarlett encounters other apprentices, each with their own clock linked to historical moments. Together, they share experiences and knowledge, exploring the unique connection they have with time. These fellow travelers become crucial allies in the quest for the enigmatic Master Clock.

Each apprentice brings a unique perspective, from the Renaissance to the French Revolution, weaving a network of temporal wisdom. Amidst laughter and debates, they face not only temporal challenges but also ethical conflicts that arise when interacting with the complexities of history. The shop, once a solitary refuge, now buzzes with the energy of a community of temporal explorers, each hoping to decipher the final secrets of time and the mythical Master Clock. The alliance, now formed, begins its journey through time. Scarlett and her fellow travelers, each with their clock linked to historical moments, contribute unique skills as they confront the complexity of adjusting clocks linked to significant events in different eras. From the Renaissance to the French Revolution, the temporal diversity of the group reflects the richness and complexity of history itself. As they venture into each adjustment, tensions arise within the group.

The responsibility of interacting with time and the uncertainty about the consequences of their actions weigh on the apprentices' shoulders. Despite the tensions, the urgent need to find answers keeps the alliance together. Each discovery, each successful adjustment, brings them one step closer to the truth

hidden behind the mysterious artifact. Master Donovan's shop, now transformed into a collective refuge for temporal explorers, resonates with the echo of laughter, passionate debates, and the shared determination to unravel the final secrets of time and the Master Clock. The alliance encounters mysterious guardians of time, entities whose existence is woven into the very fabric of temporal reality. These beings, protectors of temporal integrity, manifest as obstacles trying to impede the progress of the apprentices. Each encounter tests the loyalty and skills of the alliance members, revealing their ability to face the unknown and overcome the challenges that the quest for the Master Clock presents to them.

Scarlett, assuming the role of a leader, finds herself at a constant crossroads. Every strategic decision she makes impacts not only the group's quest but

also the internal dynamics of the alliance. Tension rises as the apprentices face ethical dilemmas, realizing that the consequences of their choices affect not only their own existence but also the very fabric of time they seek to explore and understand. Amidst these challenges, Scarlett's determination as a leader and the unique connection she shares with time become crucial in guiding the alliance through the mysterious guardians and toward the revelation of the Master Clock. In a future era, where technology and temporal complexity have reached their peak, the alliance of clockmaker apprentices discovers crucial clues leading them to the place where the Master Clock is believed to reside. Master Donovan's shop, with its collection of motionless clocks guarding centuries of shared stories, becomes the epicenter of the most intense phase of the quest.

Every step forward reveals deeper layers of knowledge about the nature of time as the apprentices confront the reality that the Master Clock is more than a simple artifact; it is a guardian of the very threads that weave the temporal tapestry. As they explore the aisles of the shop, each clock unveils its unique connection to crucial moments in history, from the Industrial Revolution to World War II and beyond. The alliance immerses itself in temporal immersion, facing more complex challenges and discovering the interconnection of their own lives with events that have shaped humanity. However, the quest also confronts the apprentices with deeper ethical dilemmas. The temptation to manipulate events for a greater good clashes with Master Donovan's persistent warning about the unforeseen consequences of playing with such powerful temporal forces. Scarlett, in her leadership role, faces difficult decisions that could alter the very essence of reality, and the alliance's loyalty is tested at every temporal crossroads.

The alliance of apprentice clockmakers prepares to face unprecedented challenges as they approach the culmination of their temporal odyssey in search of the legendary Master Clock. With the echo of lessons learned resonating in every corner of Master Donovan's shop, the apprentices arm themselves with a mix of determination and anticipation.

The truth behind this mythical artifact becomes the beacon guiding them through the complexities of history and the intricate web of time. As they enter the final phase of their quest, tensions within the alliance intensify. Divergent perspectives on the true nature of the Master Clock and how it should be used generate passionate debates. Loyalty among the apprentices is tested, as each confronts the reality of what the legendary artifact might reveal. At this critical juncture, Scarlett assumes her leadership role with a blend of confidence and caution.

The alliance embarks on a series of clock adjustments that will take them through crucial moments in history, weaving their destinies with the threads of time. The promise of revolutionary discoveries and the anxiety about unforeseen consequences propel the apprentices forward, ready to challenge not only temporal forces but also their own convictions and limitations.

Chapter 9

The Price of Knowledge

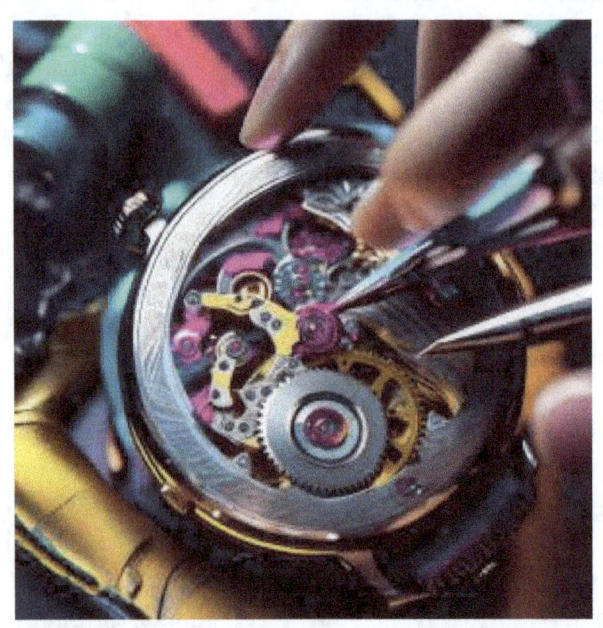

Scarlett delves even deeper into the intricate fabric of time, bringing with her the loyal alliance of apprentices who have accompanied her on this journey. Together, they explore historical moments, adjust clocks linked to crucial events, and unravel the secrets that lie within the temporal depths of each era. Each adjustment is a dance with the timelines, and Scarlett leads with a mix of determination and respect for the complexities of her role as a guardian of time. However, as her understanding of the fluidity of time deepens, Scarlett discovers that knowledge comes at a price. The consequences of her interventions in history begin to manifest in unforeseen ways, triggering a series of events that challenge not only temporal stability but also the emotional stability of the alliance. The burden of knowing what the future holds becomes more overwhelming, and Scarlett faces even more complex ethical dilemmas in her quest for the truth behind the Master Clock.

The alliance faces increasingly complex challenges, plunging into the whirlwind of intense temporal adjustments.

Scarlett, as a leader, experiences the physical and emotional burden of her role. The intensity of the adjustments leaves the young watchmaker exhausted, and the personal consequences become more evident. Scarlett is caught in involuntary temporal rifts, finding herself trapped between historical moments, an experience that tests her physical and mental endurance. The line between her present identity and her connection to time blurs, creating an internal conflict that adds to the growing tension within the alliance. The team of apprentices, witnessing Scarlett's struggle, comes together to support her, but also faces their own challenges and dilemmas.

The cohesion of the group is threatened by temporal complications, and emotions fluctuate between camaraderie and tension as they seek answers in their temporal odyssey.

The alliance, immersed in its journey through time, faces increasingly complex challenges. The intensity of temporal adjustments plunges Scarlett and her companions into a whirlwind of historical events and temporal paradoxes.

As a leader, Scarlett experiences the physical and emotional burden of her role, and the personal consequences become more evident. Involuntary temporal rifts trap her between historical moments, blurring the line between her present identity and her connection to time.

This internal conflict adds to the growing tension within the alliance. The knowledge of the Master Clock is slowly revealed, but Scarlett discovers that each answer brings new questions. The true nature of

time becomes a constantly evolving puzzle, and the quest for answers leads her to confront philosophical and conceptual dilemmas that challenge her understanding of the world.

The cohesion of the group is threatened by temporal complications, and emotions fluctuate between camaraderie and tension as they seek answers in their odyssey through time.

On a personal level, Scarlett delves into the emotional complexities of her role as a guardian of time. Each clock adjustment, though crucial to the temporal plot, leaves traces on the relationships within the alliance. Tensions rise, and the apprentices, although united by a common purpose, are affected by the emotional consequences of their interventions in the temporal fabric. Scarlett, aware that her decisions impact not only history but also interpersonal dynamics, bears the burden of knowing the fate of key individuals in history. Relationships within the alliance become increasingly strained, and the looks exchanged among members reflect the emotional complexity of their temporal journeys.

The debates intensify, and the loyalty of each apprentice is put to the test. Scarlett, as a leader, feels the weight of the difficult decisions she must make to preserve the integrity of time. Her connection with the alliance becomes a network of support and challenge, where emotions fluctuate between camaraderie and discord. In this journey through time, personal relationships intertwine with historical events, creating a complex narrative where ethical and emotional decisions intermingle in the temporal tapestry. As the alliance advances in the quest for the Master Clock, the path becomes more intricate and dangerous. Time guardians, endowed with formidable abilities, emerge as imposing obstacles challenging the alliance's determination. Scarlett, in her leadership role, faces crucial strategic decisions to overcome these challenges. Each choice carries an additional weight, as the obstacles not only threaten the mission but also further complicate the fabric of time.

The time guardians, endowed with ancestral knowledge and temporal powers, stand as protectors of temporal integrity. However, their role is shrouded in mysteries and ambiguities, creating a conflict between the alliance and these temporal custodians.

Scarlett, confronted with these enigmatic figures, is forced to navigate a delicate balance between respect for temporal rules and the pressing need to advance in her quest.

Each encounter with the time guardians leaves marks on the alliance, not only in terms of challenges overcome but also in the relationships among the apprentices. Tension grows, and Scarlett's decisions, though crucial for the mission's progression, have emotional repercussions within the group. In this journey toward the Master Clock, difficulties are not only physical but also emotional, weaving a complex plot where danger and intrigue converge in the exploration of time.

Master Donovan's shop transforms into a sanctuary for reflection and introspection. After facing the challenges and dangers in her quest for the Master Clock, Scarlett returns with heightened emotions and a mind filled with uncertainty. In this silent refuge, the clocks, witnesses to history, become mute observers of the temporal vicissitudes of the young clockmaker. Maestro Donovan, with his wise and understanding gaze, welcomes Scarlett into the heart of the shop. Aware of the cost that comes with knowledge of time, he guides his apprentice through the ethical and personal complexities that arise in her temporal journey. The mentor-apprentice relationship intensifies in this intimate space, where lessons come not only from clock adjustments but also from the profound interactions between mentor and apprentice. Scarlett finds the necessary guidance to deal with the challenges accompanying time manipulation, thus preparing herself for the deeper mysteries.

Faced with the dilemma of whether to continue or halt, Scarlett stands at a crossroads where the price of knowledge manifests in emotional scars and fractured relationships. The shop, with its clocks holding secrets and bearing the imprints of time, becomes the silent witness to Scarlett's journey. Each tick-tock of the clocks echoes the difficult decisions and personal consequences she has experienced in her quest for the Master Clock. In this temporal sanctuary, Scarlett confronts the critical decision of determining whether the knowledge of the Master Clock justifies the price she has paid and is willing to continue paying. The shop, with its atmosphere laden with mystery and reflection, becomes the refuge where Scarlett questions not only the secrets of time but also her own ethics and motivations.

Scarlett's temporal odyssey takes on a more introspective dimension, where the quest for answers intertwines with the search for herself in the intricate fabric of decisions and consequences.

Chapter 10

In Search of Atlantis

Guided by the resonances of an ancient clock, Scarlett adjusts its delicate pieces, triggering an ethereal glow that transports her to the depths of this enigmatic lost civilization. Clad in attire reflecting the splendid Atlantean era, Scarlett immerses herself in a world where magic and technology coexist in perfect harmony. Exploring the wonders and mysteries of this city, Scarlett encounters wise Atlantean leaders and curious citizens who, despite centuries passed, vividly maintain the legends of their glorious civilization. She converses with scholars unraveling the secrets of Atlantean technology and artists whose creations resonate through time.

In this magical setting, Scarlett discovers that the temporal fabric not only harbors events but also the vibrant pulse of life and creativity.

However, as she delves into the fascinating history of Atlantis, shadows of conflicts and ethical dilemmas emerge. The Atlanteans, aware of the fragility of time, share tales of difficult decisions and their consequences in the course of their civilization. The apparent harmony is tinged with internal conflicts and looming tensions, and Scarlett, as a witness to the greatness and fall of Atlantis, grapples with the duality of her duty as a temporal guardian and her desire to understand the fate of this ancient civilization. In this journey through

Atlantean mysteries, Scarlett not only uncovers the secrets of a lost society but also confronts the complexity of being a custodian of time in a world where beauty and tragedy are intertwined in the temporal tapestry.

As Scarlett interacts with the inhabitants of Atlantis, she discovers that the clock that led her here contains vital information about crucial events in Atlantean history.

Through precise adjustments, she unravels secrets buried in the annals of Atlantean time, revealing conspiracies, surprising scientific discoveries, and internal conflicts that ultimately led to the

disappearance of their civilization. The young watchmaker immerses herself in personal narratives, listening to tales of love and betrayal, sacrifice and ambition that unveil the richness of life in Atlantis. Each interaction with the Atlanteans adds new layers of complexity to the story, challenging Scarlett's perception of the linearity of time. While unraveling the mysteries lying in the past, she finds herself facing difficult ethical decisions. The knowledge gained not only sheds light on the fate of Atlantis but also raises questions about Scarlett's role as a temporal guardian. Should she intervene to change the course of events and prevent tragedy, or simply observe and learn from the past without altering it?

These ethical dilemmas stir her heart, triggering an internal struggle that plunges her even deeper into the intricate threads of Atlantean time.

The visit to Atlantis becomes a challenge for Scarlett. She is presented with the temptation to change the catastrophic fate of Atlantis, using her temporal knowledge to alter key events. However, this possibility clashes with Master Donovan's persistent warning about the unpredictable consequences of manipulating the flow of time. Scarlett finds herself at an ethical crossroads, torn between the desire to save a civilization and the responsibility to preserve temporal integrity. While exploring the grand structures and listening to the whispers of the Atlantean past, Scarlett faces decisions that could have repercussions beyond what she can imagine.

Each clock adjustment resonates with the voices of the Atlanteans, leaving the young watchmaker with the burden of deciding whether her duty as a guardian of time extends to changing the fate of a lost civilization. Scarlett's internal struggle intensifies, blending the desire to do good with the fear of triggering unintended consequences in the complex temporal dance.

Scarlett's internal conflicts intensify as Atlantis faces imminent dangers. The responsibility to maintain temporal integrity clashes with the passionate desire to help a doomed civilization. Emotional connections deepen as Scarlett immerses herself in the lives and decisions of the Atlantean inhabitants, carrying the weight of their destinies.

Faced with crucial decisions, Scarlett is forced to weigh the balance between the need to preserve the timeline and the longing to change the course of history. Imminent tragedies and the intertwined fates of the Atlanteans reveal hidden layers of the temporal fabric.

Scarlett, with her skillful hands, adjusts the clock carefully, feeling the vibration of a reality hanging in the balance. Meanwhile, the submerged city resonates with echoes of her emotions, blending the pain of loss with the hope of an altered future.

Scarlett's struggle becomes more intimate and visceral as she faces the consequences of each choice. Ethical dilemmas intertwine with emotional connections, and the fate of Atlantis hangs in the delicate balance between duty and compassion.

The exploration of Atlantis also challenges Scarlett physically and mentally. She navigates through

intricate underwater labyrinths and encounters mysterious guardians safeguarding the deepest secrets of the lost civilization. Although the alliance of apprentices is not physically present, their voices and perspectives resonate in Scarlett's mind, providing support amidst the turbulent waters of time. The connection among the apprentices manifests as an invisible yet powerful bond, strengthening Scarlett as she confronts the challenges of Atlantis. The submerged city, with its wonders and perils, becomes a stage where the young clockmaker tests her wit and courage.

Each adjustment of the clock in Atlantis reveals more layers of its history as Scarlett delves deeper into the mystery surrounding this vanished civilization. The duality between the duty to preserve temporal integrity and the desire to change Atlantis's fate manifests in the palpable tension at Scarlett's core. As the temporal odyssey progresses, Scarlett finds herself at a crossroads that extends beyond the machinations of time.

Atlantis becomes a battleground, both physically and emotionally, where each choice Scarlett makes reverberates through the ages, defining not only her journey but also the fate of a endangered civilization. Back in Maestro Donovan's shop, Scarlett brings with her the adjusted

Atlantean clock filled with knowledge. The experience in Atlantis becomes a profound reflection on the implications of her connection to time.

The submerged city leaves an indelible mark on the young clockmaker, as each adjustment of the clock reveals hidden chapters of Atlantean history. The shop, with its silent clocks, becomes a sanctuary where Scarlett reflects on her role in the vast temporal network, preparing to uncover more secrets as she continues her unique journey through the ages. The duality between the responsibility to preserve temporal integrity and the desire to intervene to change destinies intensifies. Scarlett faces an ethical dilemma that goes beyond her role as a temporal guardian. Emotions of awe and sorrow intertwine as Scarlett examines the consequences of her actions in Atlantis.

The connection with other apprentices becomes more crucial than ever as they share lessons learned and provide mutual support on this uncharted journey. Master Donovan, with his unshakable wisdom, observes Scarlett's return and senses the burden she now carries.

The shop, with its walls filled with untold stories, becomes the starting point for the next phase of Scarlett's temporal odyssey. With the Atlantean clock as her guide, she prepares to face new challenges and discoveries in her journey through the ages.

Chapter 11

Journey into
the Dark Abyss

Scarlett, after adjusting the ancient clock linked to a specific moment, finds herself transported to a romantic landscape of a bygone era. Clad in garments from another time, she encounters a fascinating character with whom she shares a deep and mysterious connection. As clock adjustments take her to different eras and places, the love between Scarlett and her mysterious beloved blossoms, defying temporal barriers. This timeless romance becomes a thread through which Scarlett experiences a full range of emotions.

The passion and joy of being with her beloved blend with the melancholy of knowing that each encounter is ephemeral within the framework of time. The relationship unfolds amidst the fluctuations of different eras, and each clock adjustment becomes a delicate balance between the desire to anchor this love in time and the understanding that temporal laws are relentless.

In each historical setting, Scarlett and her beloved face challenges that test the strength of their connection. The story of their love intertwines with key moments in history, from tumultuous wars to times of peace.

This bond, transcending the boundaries of time, becomes an emotional anchor for Scarlett, guiding her through experiences in different eras as she struggles to keep alive the flame of a love that defies the linearity of time.

However, the relationship is threatened by temporal constraints that complicate its existence. Preserving the timeline becomes a constant dilemma for Scarlett. The temptation to alter events to sustain her love haunts her, and the young clockmaker grapples between her own emotions and the

responsibility to preserve the continuity of time. Scarlett, caught between the ecstasy of timeless romance and the duty of a temporal guardian, faces even more complex challenges.

Each clock adjustment becomes an act of emotional juggling, where the need to maintain temporal integrity clashes with the desperate longing to keep her beloved in each era. Scarlett's emotions become a whirlwind, oscillating between the fleeting bliss of shared moments and the burden of the consequences that could unfold if she succumbs to the temptation to alter the natural course of time. This internal conflict adds layers of depth to the narrative, transforming Scarlett's love into a force that challenges not only temporal barriers but also the moral limitations imposed by her role as a guardian of time.

Scarlett's story becomes a fascinating balance between romantic passion and cosmic responsibility as she embarks on a journey that explores the limits of love across the ages. As Scarlett and her beloved face obstacles in different historical periods, the crucial events in which they intervene affect not only their relationship but also the entire fabric of time.

They find themselves entangled in intrigues and conflicts specific to each era, testing their love with trials that transcend temporal barriers. Scarlett's relationship becomes a narrative thread that intertwines significant moments in history, creating a complex fabric where the fate of the lovers is intrinsically linked to events influencing the surrounding reality. From the intrigues of the court of a renowned monarch to the battlefields of a world war, Scarlett and her beloved are at the epicenter of events that determine the course of humanity. Scarlett's emotions undergo a roller coaster, from the euphoria of shared moments to the despair of insurmountable challenges. The emotional burden of preserving a love through the centuries becomes the core of their journey, where passion intertwines with cosmic responsibility. This intertwining of love and duty creates a narrative rich in complexity, where each adjustment of the clock is a balancing act between passionate desire and the need to preserve the continuity of time.

The alliance of apprentices, upon learning about this special connection, provides support to Scarlett in her struggle to maintain a relationship across the eras. Although physically separated, the alliance members become a crucial pillar for Scarlett, offering insights and comfort as she navigates the complexities of temporal love. As Scarlett and her beloved face the trials of time, the alliance plays a fundamental role in their love story. Each member contributes not only technical skills to address temporal challenges but also invaluable emotional support. Conversations among apprentices become moments of reflection and advice, where they share their own experiences and perspectives on love throughout the ages. In moments of doubt and despair, the alliance becomes a refuge of solidarity, reminding Scarlett that she is not alone in her temporal journey and that others share her struggles and triumphs. Scarlett's relationship thus becomes a collective story, woven with the threads of friendship and mutual support among the apprentices.

The alliance, understanding the significance of Scarlett's special connection, not only becomes a

witness to her love through time but also an active participant in preserving this unique relationship that defies the limits of temporality.

Back in Master Donovan's shop, Scarlett reflects on the paradox of her own love story through time. Master Donovan, with his unique wisdom, guides Scarlett through the difficult decisions she must make. The shop, with its clocks that have witnessed countless stories, becomes a silent witness to a love that challenges the boundaries of temporality. Scarlett delves into contemplation of the paradoxes and challenges inherent in loving across eras.

The clock hands seem to whisper stories of lost and found loves, adding a layer of complexity to Scarlett's journey.

Master Donovan, with his knowledge accumulated over centuries, offers profound insights into the nature of love in the context of time.

The shop becomes a haven for reflection, where Scarlett and Master Donovan explore the emotional ramifications of maintaining such a unique connection. The clocks, as custodians of temporal secrets, seem to vibrate with the intensity of emotions woven into Scarlett's story. The young clockmaker faces the duality of the beauty and complexity of her temporal love, while the shop watches attentively, guarding the whispers of a romance that defies the limitations of time.

Scarlett faces a crossroads where temporal responsibility intertwine inexorably. Difficult decisions loom over her, and the young clockmaker is compelled to discover the extent to which she is willing to go for a bond that spans eras.

As she grapples with the duality of her feelings, Scarlett seeks the guidance of Master Donovan, who, with his temporal insight, provides crucial perspectives.

The shop, imbued with the energy of countless temporal stories, becomes the stage where the complexities of love and the responsibilities of a time guardian converge. Each tick-tock of the clocks seems to resonate with Scarlett's heartbeat as she contends with the inevitable tension between following the rules of time and surrendering to a love that defies the laws of temporality.

Chapter 12

The Threat of
the Paradox

Scarlett and the apprentice alliance face a crisis that threatens to unleash chaos in reality itself. Tension mounts as they detect small temporal anomalies serving as signs of an impending paradox. In the darkest corner of Master Donovan's shop, they discover a specific clock that has been inadvertently altered, triggering a series of unpredictable events. The situation becomes even more intense when they realize that the temporal paradox has deep roots in the past actions of one of the alliance members. Conflict erupts within the group as uncomfortable truths are revealed, and the bonds between the apprentices are tested. Scarlett, as the leader, finds herself at the center of the whirlwind, facing the challenging task of keeping the alliance together as they battle the forces of time. Scarlett strives to find solutions that repair the paradox without triggering even more devastating side effects

Amidst uncertainty and discord, the loyalty of the alliance is put to the test, and reality itself hangs by a thread in the hands of those striving to maintain temporal cohesion.

The time guardians, aware of the threat posed by a paradox, become relentless adversaries seeking to thwart the efforts of the apprentices. Every step the alliance takes toward resolving the paradox is hindered by the intervention of these powerful beings safeguarding the integrity of the temporal continuum.

Pressure on the alliance intensifies, and despite their unity, they experience internal tensions. Temporal responsibility clashes with the emotional bonds forged during their journey, creating a dilemma that tests the strength of their union. Scarlett, as the leader, finds herself at the epicenter of this storm, facing difficult decisions that could alter the course of their own lives and reality itself.

Emotions fluctuate between distrust and loyalty as the apprentices struggle not only against the time guardians but also against the shadows of their own past. Each encounter with the guardians becomes a test of the alliance's determination, and the possibility of failure lurks at every corner of the vast temporal tapestry they are attempting to unravel. The emotional burden on Scarlett reaches its zenith as she faces the prospect of making decisions that could impact people and events close to her heart. The dilemma intensifies as the temptation to sacrifice individual well-being for temporal stability creates internal conflicts and challenges. Scarlett, torn between her duty as a guardian of time and her personal connections, experiences an emotional storm as she contemplates the implications of her

choices. The pressure to maintain alliance cohesion adds to her distress as tensions rise among the apprentices, each dealing with their own internal struggles.

Master Donovan, with his unique wisdom, guides Scarlett and the alliance through the complexities of correcting the paradox. The shop becomes a refuge where Scarlett reflects on the impending temporal imbalance, pondering the implications of her actions on the continuity of time and the relationships she has cultivated. At this crucial moment, emotions surface as Scarlett faces the possibility of sacrificing her own happiness for the sake of temporal stability. Tensions within the alliance intensify as each apprentice grapples with the duality between their duty as guardians of time and their personal connections.

The emotional burden of the decision is reflected in the worried faces of alliance members, and the uncertainty of the outcome adds a veil of anxiety to the atmosphere. The alliance, forged across eras, faces a definitive test that will challenge not only their temporal skills but also the strength of their bonds and the integrity of their decisions.

Scarlett and the alliance work tirelessly to rectify the mistake before the paradox unleashes irreversible havoc on reality. The tension in Master Donovan's shop is palpable, with clocks seemingly whispering the urgency of the moment.

The alliance, united by the need to correct the temporal imbalance, faces unexpected challenges as the time guardians, aware of the threat, deploy more formidable obstacles. The emotional burden for Scarlett reaches its zenith, as tough decisions force her to weigh temporal responsibility against the personal connections she has   forged. The dilemma intensifies, and each clock adjustment becomes a juggling act between preserving temporal continuity and safeguarding emotional bonds. The alliance faces a definitive test that will define its legacy in the very fabric of time, and the uncertainty of the outcome adds an additional dimension to the complexity of their efforts.

Chapter 13

Awakening in the Middle Ages

Scarlett skillfully adjusts an ancient clock linked to the Middle Ages in Master Donovan's shop. The magic of the clock envelops Scarlett, and suddenly, she finds herself immersed in the vibrant setting of the Middle Ages. Surrounded by majestic castles, bustling markets, and knights in shining armor, Scarlett delves into the unique atmosphere of this era. While adjusting the clock, Scarlett encounters captivating characters, from benevolent nobles to shrewd merchants and brave knights. The complexity of medieval society unfolds through interactions and conflicts that challenge modern perceptions of justice and honor.

The precise adjustments of the clock not only transport Scarlett through time but also immerse her in the intrigues and challenges specific to this historical period.

The decisions she makes and the relationships she forges will impact not only her personal experience but also the broader tapestry of medieval history. As Scarlett navigates through these crucial events, the duality of her role as an observer and a participant becomes increasingly evident, generating emotional tensions.

Scarlett encounters wise alchemists who, over the centuries, have guarded ancestral knowledge. These masters reveal hidden secrets to Scarlett that have had a profound impact on events throughout history, demonstrating that alchemy not only transforms elements but can also influence the very flow of time. Each revelation awakens in Scarlett a deeper understanding of the interconnection between alchemy and her own mission as a guardian of time. These teachings challenge her perceptions and propel her to explore the possibility of using alchemy as a tool to maintain temporal balance.

The relationships Scarlett develops with these alchemists, marked by trust and collaboration, become emotional anchors in her journey through the eras. The wisdom shared by these characters not only enriches her understanding of alchemy but also adds unexpected dimensions to her connection with time. As Scarlett delves into alchemical teachings, she faces ethical dilemmas and moral decisions that challenge her role as a guardian of the temporal continuum. Scarlett comes across an ancient prophecy related to alchemy; it warns that certain adjustments to the clocks linked to the Middle Ages could trigger events with monumental consequences for the future.

The prophecy, with its cryptic words, adds an additional layer of mystery to the temporal plot. Scarlett is confronted with the responsibility of

handling this delicate information and wrestles with whether she should intervene to change the fate of the coming eras.

The uncertainty of the future becomes a persistent shadow over her decisions as Scarlett navigates the crossroads between her duty as a guardian of time and the temptation to alter the temporal flow to prevent potential catastrophes. The characters surrounding her, from ancient alchemists to those guarding the prophecy, share their own perspectives and ethical challenges. Interpersonal relationships become tense as the alliance of apprentices debates the most appropriate course of action. At this crossroads, Scarlett faces the loneliness of her role, making crucial decisions that will resonate in the fabric of time. Immersed in the vibrant scene of the Middle Ages, Scarlett interacts with monarchs, sorcerers, and knights, each with their own agendas and visions of the future. The halls of castles resonate with conspiracies and whispers of intrigue as Scarlett navigates through this complex social tapestry. Monarchs, eager to consolidate their power, and sorcerers, with their hidden knowledge, add layers of complexity to the temporal narrative.

Scarlett finds herself amidst power games that threaten to alter the course of known history and challenge her ability to preserve temporal integrity. Knights, loyal to their lords, can also become allies or adversaries in this journey. Scarlett must discern between loyalties and motivations as she faces decisions that go beyond clock adjustments, impacting the very fabric of time itself. Each conversation and choice takes on a crucial nuance, and emotions intensify as Scarlett becomes involved in the dramas and conflicts of an era where honor and betrayal are as intrinsic as the temporal complexities she faces. Immersed in the magic and alchemy of the Middle Ages, Scarlett experiences a unique connection with these elements. Her ability to understand and manipulate magic places her in a unique position in this mystical society, where alchemists and sorcerers value her exceptional skills. However, this privileged position also exposes her to risks and unexpected challenges.

The temptation to use magic to influence events becomes a constant dilemma for Scarlett. As she discovers ancient prophecies and hidden secrets, she faces crucial decisions on how to employ her magical knowledge. The internal struggle between the desire to change the course of events and Master Donovan's constant warning about the unpredictable consequences of interfering with time intensifies. Scarlett must balance her magical abilities with the responsibility to preserve temporal continuity, confronting ethical challenges that will test her determination and understanding of the temporal fabric.

Although the apprentices' alliance is not physically present, its influence extends significantly into history. Through temporal messages and special connections, Scarlett's companions remain an essential part of her journey in the Middle Ages. Familiar voices provide support and guidance at crucial moments, strengthening the bond between the apprentices despite temporal barriers.

Back in the shop, Master Donovan observes Scarlett's return with interest. As she reflects on the events, Scarlett faces fundamental questions about the role of magic and alchemy in the evolution of history. Master Donovan, with his insightful gaze, perceives Scarlett's internal tensions and guides her wisely through the complexities of her unique connection to time. The shop, with its clocks witnessing changes in the temporal tide, guards the secrets of a medieval era that has left an indelible mark on Scarlett's temporal narrative. The young watchmaker immerses herself in reflection, questioning how medieval events affect the very fabric of time.

The apprentices' alliance, although physically separated, remains a crucial pillar. Through temporal messages and special connections, Scarlett's companions provide support and guidance as she navigates the mysteries and dangers of the Middle Ages.

Master Donovan, with his profound understanding of temporality, points out that each era has its own essence and contributes to the complete tapestry of time. Scarlett, with the adjusted clock in hand, prepares to unravel more secrets as she continues her journey through the ages, exploring the complexities of magic, alchemy, and human connections that transcend temporal boundaries.

Chapter 14

The Conclave
of the Clocks

The summoning to the Conclave of the Clocks, a transcendental gathering of temporal guardians and ancestral timepieces, reveals deeper layers of Scarlett's role in the temporal balance. As she immerses herself in this unique assembly, Scarlett faces challenges that surpass anything experienced thus far. The tension between temporal responsibility and her desire to comprehend the mysteries of time intensifies. The leaders of the Conclave, imposing figures with centuries of experience, closely watch Scarlett's decisions, aware that her role in the temporal plot is becoming more crucial with each clock adjustment. Scarlett, carefully adjusting an ancestral clock in Master Donovan's shop, where magic permeates the air. An ethereal glow fills the room as a temporal portal opens before her, transporting her to a mysterious place where ancient clocks line a majestic hall. Each clock represents a crucial fragment of the temporal fabric and is linked to significant historical moments.

The Conclave of the Clocks, composed of temporal guardians from past and future eras, receives her with solemnity. Scarlett, aware that her presence is no coincidence, faces enigmatic figures who understand the intricacies of time. As she interacts with these ancestral beings, she discovers that every choice she has made so far has resonated throughout the timeline, affecting those who have shared her journey and the very reality itself. The emotional weight of these revelations envelops her, but her determination to understand the purpose behind her connection to time intensifies. The leaders of the Conclave, with wisdom accumulated over the centuries, reveal that Scarlett is an essential participant.

Her ability to adjust the ancestral clocks makes her a guardian of temporal balance. However, this revelation is accompanied by even greater challenges, as she must face the responsibility of preserving temporal continuity while unraveling the secrets of her own destiny intertwined with the fabric of time.

The Conclave of the Clocks is a monumental assembly, a gathering of time guardians from various eras. Scarlett encounters guardians of clocks linked to moments from distant epochs to the distant future. Each one shares their unique wisdom about the influence of those moments on the overall temporal plot. This scenario provides Scarlett with an unprecedented insight into the vastness and complexity of the temporal network. Among the guardians, one stands out with a century-old clock emitting a mystical glow. This elderly guardian, with eyes that have witnessed countless sunrises, reveals to Scarlett details about her own crucial role in the preservation of time. Interactions with these guardians are not only informative but also emotional. Scarlett experiences a deep connection with her predecessors and successors, sharing the weight of being guardians of time. As the Conclave progresses, tensions and conflicts among the guardians are revealed, each advocating for the importance of their respective key moments.

The diversity of perspectives and agendas generates heated debates about the direction the timeline should take. Scarlett is immersed in this temporal conflict, where it is not only about preserving the past but also about forging a coherent and harmonious future. At the epicenter of the Conclave, Scarlett faces transcendent decisions that will affect the stability of reality itself. The emotional burden intensifies as she is forced to balance loyalty to her own era and to those with whom she has shared her temporal journey. Her role as a guardian of temporal balance places her at the center of a dilemma that will determine the fate of the temporal network and those who depend on her intervention.

As she interacts with the guardians and explores the chamber, Scarlett discovers the complexity of her role as a guardian of time. Philosophical discussions about intervening in historical events and the responsibility to safeguard the temporal flow immerse her in passionate debates.

Revelations about the interconnections of historical events and the influence of individual guardians raise fundamental questions about the nature of time and destiny. Each guardian has a unique and profound story, marked by the choices they made in their respective eras. Scarlett becomes immersed in the emotions and experiences of these guardians, understanding the burden they carry. Among them, an ancient warrior who witnessed epic battles, a scholar whose discoveries transformed entire civilizations, and an artist whose work endured the passage of time as a testament to human creativity. The relationships among the guardians become complex as they disagree on their opinions about temporal intervention. Some advocate for preserving history as it is, while others suggest adjustments to improve the course of humanity. Scarlett finds herself caught in the middle of these debates, questioning her own convictions and facing moral dilemmas that challenge her understanding of right and wrong in the context of temporal manipulation.

The Conclave becomes a crucible of emotions and conflicts, where every spoken word and every decision made reverberate through the chamber like ripples in the fabric of time. The emotional burden reaches its peak, and Scarlett stands at a crossroads that will change not only her perspective on time but also her connection with the entire temporal network. During the conclave, forgotten prophecies are unraveled, and events that could significantly alter the course of time are discussed. Scarlett faces emotional challenges as she discovers the magnitude of her role and the consequences of each choice in her temporal odyssey.

The revelation of her specific role in the temporal balance marks a crucial point in her understanding of the vast temporal network and its impact on her. Ancient and mysterious prophecies paint an intriguing picture of Scarlett's role in crucial events that have yet to take place.

As visions of the future intertwine with her present, the emotional burden intensifies, and Scarlett stands at a crossroads, torn between following a predetermined destiny or forging her own path in the temporal network. The conclave also reveals the existence of oscillating forces that threaten to unbalance the temporal network. A dark entity, beyond the laws governing time, emerges as a tangible threat. The alliance of apprentices, despite their experience and skills, faces an adversary whose motives and methods defy conventional understanding of temporal travel.

Scarlett, enveloped in the tension of these revelations, must confront her own destiny and make decisions that will not only affect her future but the very fate of temporal reality itself. The conclave hall becomes a stage of conflicting emotions, moral conflicts, and the inevitable clash of forces that will determine the course of time in the upcoming chapters of her journey. The progress of the conclave is not without dangers.

External forces, including rebellious guardians and temporal entities, seek to exploit the shared knowledge for their own purposes. Scarlett, with her temporal prowess and keen perception, detects the shadows looming over the conclave. The responsibility to protect timeless wisdom falls on her shoulders, and tensions rise as infiltration attempts by external forces intensify. The apprentice alliance, despite their dedication, faces formidable challenges as they combat those who seek to distort the temporal flow to fulfill their own designs. Amidst these conflicts, emotions flow like turbulent temporal currents.

Loyalty is tested, and alliances among the guardians are forged and broken in the crucible of tensions. Scarlett, aware of the delicate balance that upholds reality, finds herself in a unique position to lead

the defense of the conclave, facing not only tangible threats but also dilemmas that test her commitment to the preservation of time.

The conclave, initially promising a gathering of shared knowledge, transforms into a battlefield where temporal destinies and emotions collide. Revelations and betrayals weave a complex plot that will shape Scarlett's future and her relationship with the temporal network. Her decisions and actions, from this point forward, will not only impact her own story but also the very destiny of temporal reality. Back in the shop, Scarlett reflects on the conclave's revelations and prepares to face the challenges in her ongoing odyssey through time.

Chapter 15

Confrontation with
an Ancestral Enemy

Scarlett faces an epic challenge as the ancestral enemy with ambitions to control time is revealed. Scarlett becomes the last barrier between this enemy and the integrity of the temporal fabric. Scarlett, the fearless leader of the apprentice alliance, is immersed in detecting unsettling signs of temporal anomalies alongside her team. While examining temporal records, a coded and mysterious message emerges, warning of the emergence of an ancestral enemy. This being threatens to unleash chaos in the very structure of time, a danger that arouses deep fears among the guardians of time. As the alliance delves into the investigation, tensions escalate. Each apprentice feels the burden of responsibility and the urgency of the situation. Uncertainty about the identity and motivations of the unknown enemy adds an element of intrigue.

In their quest, they discover crucial events in the fabric of time that could be linked to the imminent confrontation. Emotions fluctuate between anxiety and courage as the apprentices prepare to face an enemy that defies the very laws of temporality. Scarlett, the courageous leader of the apprentice alliance, immerses herself in an investigation that takes her through various historical moments. Armed with her temporal expertise, she traces the traces left by the ancestral enemy, unraveling manipulations and distortions that have affected crucial events throughout history. In her journey, she discovers that these alterations manifest as temporal rifts, visible manifestations of the fragility of the temporal fabric.

Every step Scarlett takes into the past reveals perplexing details about the enemy's machinations. She encounters events that have been subtly altered, leaving disruptive ripples in the flow of time.

The magnitude of these manipulations translates into distortions in reality itself, creating ephemeral alternative worlds that threaten to collapse at any moment. The team of apprentices experiences the immediacy of the consequences, confronting altered realities and defying the fundamental laws of time. Temporal rifts become gateways to bewildering and often dangerous scenarios. The imminent threat of a temporal catastrophe looms over them, generating a palpable urgency in every action. In her role as a leader, Scarlett guides her team with determination through these challenges, facing not only temporal adversity but also the intense emotions that arise when the stability of the past, present, and future is threatened. The long-awaited final confrontation finally materializes in a timeless place, a corner of the universe where temporal lines converge. Here, the ancestral enemy reveals itself as a formidable force, surrounded by the very essence of temporality.

Scarlett, with determination and courage, comes face to face with this ancestral being, whose presence exudes profound knowledge of the secrets of time. The atmosphere is charged with tension as the two antagonistic forces confront each other. The ancestral figure, shrouded in an aura of mystery, unfolds its ambition to control time. This ambition, threatening and defiant, manifests as a direct and ominous threat to the temporal continuity everyone knows.

The confrontation unfolds as a duel where not only temporal skills and knowledge are at stake but also fundamental philosophies about the nature of time and destiny. Scarlett, the defender of temporal stability, is forced to confront not only the cunning of her enemy but also profound questions about the balance between temporal control and freedom. The showdown unfolds in a surrealistic setting, where the past, present, and future intertwine in a tumultuous dance.

In this epic confrontation, shocking truths are unveiled, and the limits of reality are explored, leading the characters to a stunning and revealing climax. At the zenith of the confrontation, Scarlett faces challenges that go beyond mere physical struggle. The ancestral figure, in its attempt to destabilize her, deploys emotional tactics. It seeks to persuade her, not only with the threat of its temporal power but also with tempting promises to change personal events and alter individual destinies.

At this critical moment, Scarlett finds herself at an emotional crossroads. The temptation to yield to the possibility of redeeming painful pasts or shaping desired futures haunts her.

The promise of temporal control that could alleviate her personal suffering entices her, but her commitment to temporal responsibility and the integrity of time acts as anchors that keep her steadfast.

This internal conflict adds layers of depth to her character, revealing her courage in resisting temptations that could shatter the very foundations of time. The confrontation thus becomes a test not only of skills but also of l integrity in the tumultuous stage of temporality. During the confrontation, the apprentice alliance emerges as a crucial factor, playing both a tactical and emotional role in the conflict. Though physically distant, they maintain a connection through temporal messages, providing Scarlett with vital perspectives and strategies to confront the ancestral enemy.

In this support network, the unity of the alliance becomes an essential element. They face obstacles and challenges posed by this ancient threat with a synchronization that reflects the strength of their temporal bond. This strategic and emotional intertwining not only reinforces the narrative but also underscores the importance of collaboration in the fight against an enemy that defies the very norms of time.

Scarlett, in a breathtaking display, unleashes all her temporal knowledge and skills forged throughout her journey. The battle extends beyond the limits of reality, encompassing various historical moments and temporal dimensions. This conflict not only challenges the conventional perception of linear time but also redefines the limits of reality itself. The resolution of this confrontation not only determines the fate of Scarlett and her loyal alliance but also carries far-reaching implications for the very structure of time. Every move and strategy of Scarlett resonates beyond the battle, marking a milestone in temporal history. Back in Master Donovan's shop, Scarlett reflects on the lessons learned and the consequences of the confrontation with the ancestral enemy. The shop, with its silent clocks, holds the secrets of this epic temporal battle that will leave an indelible mark on Scarlett's narrative as she continues her journey through time.

Chapter 16

The Revelation
of the Master Clock

Scarlett faces a monumental challenge as she follows temporal clues and signals leading her to the sacred location of the Master Clock. On this journey, she encounters various time guardians attempting to impede her progress, each presenting trials that test her courage and wisdom acquired throughout her temporal odyssey. Temporal traps intertwine with the mystical architecture of the path to the Master Clock, and each step involves crucial decisions that will impact not only her personal destiny but also the temporal balance. Feeling the intensity of the forces at play, Scarlett confronts moral dilemmas and philosophical challenges that question her understanding of time and her role as a guardian.

The guardians she encounters not only pose physical obstacles but also represent conceptual barriers that challenge her fundamental beliefs.

Scarlett's courage is tested at every crossroads, and her determination strengthens as she ventures into the unknown, eager to uncover the deepest secrets of the Master Clock and the implications they hold for reality itself.

On this journey, a rich blend of emotions unfolds, from uncertainty to unwavering determination. Upon reaching the sanctuary of the Master Clock, Scarlett is impressed by the majesty of the room, where a collection of clocks emits an ethereal glow. At the center stands the Master Clock, whose gears turn with a resonance that seems to transcend time itself. Feeling the intensity of the place, Scarlett understands that she is at the crossroads of all eras.

The room is enveloped in a mystical atmosphere, where the flow of time converges at a central point, manifesting as a cosmic dance of lights and shadows.

As Scarlett approaches the Master Clock, the voices of the time guardians from the past, present, and

future resonate in her ears, providing her with a unique perspective on the vastness of the temporal network. Each clock in the room tells a story, and the whispers of the gears reveal crucial events, transcendent decisions, and the intertwined destinies of those who have manipulated time.. Internal conflicts and past decisions take on new meaning in this temporal epicenter. The Master Clock room becomes a space where threads of destiny intertwine, and Scarlett, confronting the accumulated knowledge of all eras, prepares to uncover the truth behind the temporal network and her fundamental role in its preservation. The confrontation with the Master Clock unfolds as a pivotal moment. This entity, imbued with the essence of time itself, reveals shocking truths. Scarlett discovers that her connection to time goes beyond being a guardian; she is considered a vital piece in the temporal balance.

Resonances from the past, present, and future intertwine around her, creating a temporal symphony that only she can comprehend. The Master Clock unveils to Scarlett details about her origin, highlighting specific events in her life that have shaped her as a crucial force in the temporal storyline. Every decision, every adjustment of the clock, has been part of a broader cosmic narrative. The weight of responsibility on Scarlett's shoulders intensifies as she realizes that her journey is not just a personal quest but a cosmic dance weaving the destinies of all. Scarlett's emotions fluctuate between awe and overwhelming responsibility.

The Master Clock chamber becomes a reflection of her own journey, where the past, present, and future converge at a focal point. Scarlett, now aware of her crucial role, prepares to make decisions that will not only impact her own destiny but the very integrity of the temporal network she has sworn to protect.

As she explores this new understanding of herself, she faces the overwhelming responsibility of her role in maintaining temporal balance. The deepening of her connection to time comes with unexpected risks and sacrifices. The Master Clock chamber vibrates with an energy that mirrors Scarlett's tumultuous emotions. The young clockmaker, now infused with the essence of time, delves into profound reflection on the meaning of her existence and the implications of her actions on the temporal network. Scarlett, torn between fascination and apprehension, grapples with the duality of her nature. On one hand, she feels uplifted by the cosmic significance of her role; on the other hand, the burden of responsibility threatens to overwhelm her. The confrontation with the Master Clock not only unveils cosmic truths but also unleashes a whirlwind of emotions in the protagonist, pushing her to the limits of her emotional and mental capacities.

Guided by the unique wisdom of the Master Clock, Scarlett experiences temporal visions that reveal crucial events in past and future history. Forgotten prophecies are unveiled, and discussions about the destinies of entire civilizations fill the chamber. Scarlett immerses herself in an experience that challenges the linearity of time, understanding that each clock adjustment and choice has ramifications across the vast temporal network. As she witnesses the threads of destiny intertwining before her, she confronts the magnitude of her role as the guardian of time.

The duality of knowledge and responsibility manifests in her expression, revealing the emotional weight that accompanies cosmic wisdom. The visions, like fragments of a temporal tapestry, paint pictures of past and future events. Scarlett, woven into the very fabric of time, becomes both a witness and a participant in the temporal epic.

Each revelation resonates with an emotional echo that oscillates between wonder and concern for the fate of those she has known and loved throughout her temporal odyssey. The experience in the Master Clock chamber stands as a foundational pillar in Scarlett's evolution as a custodian of time, defining her destiny as she grapples with the complexity of the temporal network that weaves her existence. Scarlett's internal conflict reaches its climax. Faced with difficult decisions and the weight of her destiny, the temptation to alter events for a greater good clash with the Master Clock's warnings about unforeseeable consequences. Scarlett, at the epicenter of a temporal storm, is engulfed in ethical dilemmas that surpass any previous temporal challenge. The Master Clock chamber, saturated with the magnitude of time, becomes the stage for her internal struggle. The fates of those she loves hang in the balance as the responsibility to preserve temporal integrity clashes with her passionate desires.

Every word from the Master Clock resonates in her mind, raising fundamental questions about free will, divine intervention, and the unpredictability of fate. Enshrouded in the dimness of the chamber, Scarlett stands on the threshold of a choice that will alter the very structure of time. Determination reflect in her eyes as she decides between following the predestined course or challenging cosmic rules for the sake of those she loves. Back in Master Donovan's shop, Scarlett carries with her the revelations of the Master Clock.

Chapter 17

Sacrifices for Balance

Scarlett and the apprentice alliance confront a temporal imbalance that threatens to unleash chaos across various eras. They are forced to act swiftly in response to temporal signals indicating the urgency of intervention. Scarlett, aware of the responsibility she carries, embarks on a series of strategic clock adjustments. Each choice carries significant weight, as the consequences will impact not only the overall temporal plot but also her personal life. The Master Clock room is filled with palpable tension as Scarlett considers the possibilities. Her trembling hands carefully manipulate the mechanisms of the ancient clocks, feeling the pulse of time beneath her fingers. With each adjustment, visions of the past and future unfold before her eyes. The emotional burden of witnessing crucial events, lost loves, and imminent tragedies envelops her.

Scarlett faces the dilemma of balancing the common good with the emotional bonds she has forged throughout her journey. The responsibility of being the guardian of time becomes an unbearable burden, but her determination persists. Each decision brings her closer to resolution but also distances her from the simplicity of a life without the burden of temporality. In this transcendent moment, Scarlett finds herself at the crossroads of her destiny, willing to sacrifice her own happiness for the stability of reality itself. Scarlett's internal conflict intensifies as she makes decisions that involve personal sacrifices. She is forced to give up close relationships, cherished experiences, and, in some cases, her own emotional stability. The ethical burden becomes increasingly heavy, and Scarlett is in a constant struggle between the need to maintain temporal continuity and preserve her own humanity.

Each clock adjustment, though vital for temporal balance, leaves emotional scars on Scarlett's heart. The images of what could have been, but now fades in the temporal stream, haunt her. Despite her dedication to the cause, Scarlett faces the harsh reality of difficult decisions and the inevitable losses that accompany them. In this emotional journey, she discovers not only the complexity of time but also the fragility of human connections.

As the internal conflict intensifies, Scarlett faces the possibility of losing herself in the process of maintaining temporal balance, questioning the true nature of her mission and how far she is willing to sacrifice for the sake of reality itself. The apprentice alliance, though united in purpose, faces internal tensions. Scarlett's decisions generate controversies challenges within the group. While

some members of the alliance insist on the need to preserve the continuity of time at any cost, others question the ethics of sacrificing individuals and significant events for the sake of temporal stability.

These disagreements not only reflect different perspectives but also reveal the inherent complexities of the task of being guardians of time. Tension rises as the ramifications of the decisions made and the unexpected consequences that arise are explored. Scarlett, as the leader of the alliance, finds herself at the epicenter of these conflicts. Her ability to maintain the group's cohesion becomes a monumental task as she must balance the ethical demands of her peers with the urgent need to protect temporal stability. Scarlett is confronted with the need for a significant personal sacrifice. The choice she makes not only impacts the structure of time but also redefines her own journey and destiny. The battle between temporal responsibility and emotional connections reaches its climax, leaving Scarlett marked by emotional scars as she moves towards. The emotional weight of the decision is reflected in Scarlett's transformation, whose eyes carry the burden of the eras she has touched.

Loss and sacrifice, inevitable elements on the path of a time guardian, intertwine with the fabric of the story, adding layers of complexity and depth to Scarlett's character. As she progresses, Scarlett finds herself at a crossroads between duty and desire, where the cost of being the guardian of time manifests not only in historical events but also in the very fabric of her being. The narrative delves into the nuances of difficult decisions and their repercussions, taking the reader on an emotional journey that challenges expectations and explores the intrinsic nature of choices in Scarlett's temporal storyline. Back in Master Donovan's shop, Scarlett carries the indelible traces of sacrifices made for

temporal balance. The shop, with its silent clocks, becomes a haven where Scarlett reflects on tough decisions and the personal cost of her role as the guardian of time. The uncertainty of the future persists, and the clocks, though silent, bear witness to the aftermath of sacrifices made in pursuit of temporal stability.

The clocks, silent witnesses to history, record the emotional weight carried by Scarlett as the guardian of time. The shop, which has witnessed countless stories throughout the ages, becomes a sanctuary where Scarlett finds comfort and strength to move forward. Each tick-tock of the clocks tells the tale of sacrifices and determination, reminding Scarlett of the significance of her role in the intricate dance of time.

Chapter 18

The Redemption
of the Enemy

Scarlett, following the signals that lead her to a timeless place in a unique corner, where the ancestral enemy awaits. Instead of the expected hostility, the atmosphere is charged with resonant emotions and unexpected revelations. The ancestral enemy, whose name and past are now laid bare, shares a tragic story marked by losses, sufferings, and difficult choices. Through temporal visions, Scarlett experiences the events that led this entity down the dark path of temporal control. Empathy wells within her as she understands the complex motivations and deep wounds that drove the ancestral enemy to seek power over time. In the visions, Scarlett finds herself in the crucial moments that determined the fate of the ancestral enemy. She discovers the betrayals suffered, opportunities lost, and heartbreaking tragedies that forged a hardened will.

As Scarlett witnesses these events, the line between ally and enemy blurs. complexities emerge, and the young guardian is confronted with the inherent duality of human nature. Emotion mixes with surprise as she understands that the ancestral enemy, at an earlier moment, shared a similar purpose to hers: the preservation of the temporal fabric. The revelation of the ancestral enemy's history adds layers of depth to the narrative, challenging previous perceptions and raising questions about redemption and forgiveness. Scarlett, now armed with a more complete knowledge, faces the titanic task of reconciling her role as a guardian with the possibility of redeeming the ancestral enemy. The clocks, as silent witnesses, seem to vibrate with the intensity of the revelations. Master Donovan, with his wise gaze, guides Scarlett in assimilating this new perspective and prepares her for the imminent challenges that lie ahead in her temporal odyssey.

Scarlett's internal conflict intensifies as the lines between good and evil blur. Decisions become more complicated, and Scarlett faces the challenging task of reconciling the previous image of the enemy with the revealed truth. The complexity, raising questions about free will, redemption, and the inherently graphic nature of time, plunges her into a whirlwind of emotions. The duality of the human condition is reflected in her own internal struggle as she strives to find a balance between temporal responsibility and compassionate understanding towards the ancestral enemy.

The apprentice alliance, initially skeptical and cautious, also experiences internal dissonance. Tensions arise as group members grapple with the revelation of the ancestral enemy's past. Each apprentice confronts the duality between the desire

for justice and the possibility of redemption, generating internal conflicts and intense debates within the alliance.

The weight of the truth alters previous dynamics, challenging loyalties and trust among the apprentices. Unexpected alliances are forged as each confronts the reality that, even in time, the lines between hero and villain can blur. Scarlett finds herself at a crossroads where she must choose between forgiving the ancestral enemy or condemning them for their past actions. The battle is not just a clash of temporal skills but a philosophical collision that challenges fundamental notion of redemption. Emotions swirl within her as she reflects on the complexity of judging someone whose past is presented as stained with suffering and loss. The duality between compassion and the need to protect temporal integrity creates an internal conflict that resonates in every choice Scarlett must make. At this crossroads, the young watchmaker confronts not only her enemy but the shadows of her own challenging decisions that have led her to this critical moment in her temporal odyssey.

The quest for redemption becomes a key factor, Scarlett, now faced with the responsibility of making ethically significant decisions, confronts an uncertain future as she continues her journey through time. The moral complexity of forgiving the ancestral enemy, whose story reveals layers of suffering and pain, is intertwined with the challenge of balancing justice and mercy in the temporal fabric. The uncertainty of destiny is reflected in the clocks of Master Donovan's shop, which remain silent as Scarlett engages in reflection.

At this crucial moment, the emotions of the young watchmaker intertwine with the currents of time, creating a narrative rich in nuances and unexpected twists. Redemption, as a guiding thread, weaves an emotional plot that challenges not only Scarlett but also the very foundations of temporality she seeks to protect. Scarlett confronts the complexity of reconciling the need for justice.

Back in Maestro Donovan's shop, Scarlett reflects on the complexities and implications of the ancestral enemy's redemption. The shop, with its witnessing clocks, holds the secrets of this unexpected evolution in the temporal narrative, marking a milestone in Scarlett's journey and her perception of good and evil on the vast tapestry of time.

Chapter 19

The Final Adjustment

Guided by the teachings of the Master Clock and the experiences accumulated throughout her odyssey, Scarlett carefully examines the clocks lining the shelves of the shop. Her eyes settle on a central clock that seems to resonate with the very essence of time. This clock, linked to crucial moments in history, reveals itself as the key to carrying out the ultimate adjustment. The room fills with a mystical energy as Scarlett initiates the process, and a temporal portal opens before her, taking her on afinal journey through the vastness of time. Upon crossing the portal, Scarlett finds herself in a timeless place where temporal lines converge in a dazzling display of past, present, and future events. Here, at this culminating point of her temporal journey, the young watchmaker faces a crossroads where redemption and responsibility converge in a unique amalgamation.

As she adjusts the clock linked to the essence of time, visions of crucial moments and past decisions flow before her eyes, reminding her of the journey that has brought her here. In this final stretch of her voyage, Scarlett encounters past and future versions of herself, each reflecting different choices and sacrifices made in the name of temporal balance. Emotions converge in a whirlwind as Scarlett confronts her own humanity and that of those she has encountered on her journey.

The dilemma of forgiving the ancestral enemy takes on new dimensions, and Scarlett finds herself at a moral crossroads, feeling the weight of each choice she has made. The temporal portal, witness to this critical moment, vibrates with the intensity of the decisions being made. Scarlett, enveloped in the essence of time, delves into a profound reflection on the meaning of her journey and the responsibility she carries as the guardian of time.

The final adjustment takes Scarlett through various historical moments and temporal dimensions. Each adjustment is an intense challenge, with tests designed to assess her temporal wisdom and her ability to balance the crucial elements of time. Every choice she makes, every turn of the gear, has immediate and long-term repercussions, and the pressure to determine the fate of the clocks and time itself weighs on her shoulders. Scarlett finds herself adjusting clocks linked to transcendent events, from the formation of ancient civilizations to crucial moments in the evolution of humanity.

Each adjustment immerses her in the intensity of those moments, allowing her to feel the emotions, dilemmas, and joys that have shaped history. Scarlett's unique connection to the essence of time guides her through these adjustments, but it also exposes her to the complexities and nuances of human experiences throughout the eras.

As she progresses in her task, Scarlett encounters key figures from different eras, some of whom have left indelible marks on the temporal narrative. Dialogues with these characters reveal hidden aspects

of historical events, as well as their own challenges and sacrifices in the name of temporal balance. In this final journey, Scarlett is not just an observer of history but an active participant who influences the very flow of time. The temptations to alter events for a greater good clash with the constant warning from the Master Clock about the unforeseen consequences of tampering with time. Scarlett is forced to confront monumental dilemmas, where each adjustment has ramifications that extend across the vast temporal network.

The ethical burden becomes even more pressing as Scarlett's decisions impact not only historical events but also the lives of individuals and the integrity of reality itself.

Scarlett's internal conflict reaches a climax as she grapples with the balance between the desire to change the course of history and the need to respect the limits of time. Emotional tension intensifies, leading Scarlett to confront not only external challenges but also internal dilemmas that test her courage and determination in her role as the guardian of time.

Through temporal messages and special connections, Scarlett's companions provide support and guidance as she faces the final adjustment. Each member of the alliance, despite not being physically present, becomes an essential part of the temporal narrative, contributing wisdom, experiences, and unique connections. Tensions and emotions run high in Master Donovan's shop, where the alliance gathers, eagerly awaiting the critical outcome of Scarlett's efforts. The uncertainty of the future, combined with the deep emotional bond among the apprentices, creates an atmosphere charged with anticipation and apprehension.

In the room, the watches that bear witness to Scarlett's temporal journey maintain an expectant silence, as if holding the collective breath of reality itself. Each tick-tock resonates like an echo of the decisions Scarlett faces in her mission. Meanwhile, temporal messages from the alliance offer words of encouragement, reminding her of the importance of her role and the trust they have placed in her. The narrative weaves through emotional bonds, crucial events, and the imminent conclusion of the final adjustment, creating a blend of suspense, camaraderie, and determination that propels Scarlett toward the culmination of her epic temporal odyssey. The room glows with a dazzling light as time itself seems to stand still. Each turn of the gear is a palpable expression of the responsibility Scarlett carries on her shoulders.

In this transcendent moment, the resolution of her final adjustment will determine the fate of the watches and, ultimately, the temporal balance as a whole.

The atmosphere is charged with intensity, and Scarlett faces the crossroads between the need to preserve temporal continuity and the immediate consequences that her choices may bring. The internal battle between temporal responsibility and immediate repercussions reaches its peak, leaving the question hanging in the air of whether Scarlett can find the delicate balance necessary to guide the narrative of time to a satisfactory conclusion. Back in Master Donovan's shop, Scarlett reflects on the final adjustment and the consequences of her actions. The room, with its silent watches, holds the secrets of this ultimate experience and marks the end of Scarlett's temporal odyssey. Each tick-tock seems to resonate with the crucial decisions made and the ramifications of her choices. Facing the uncertainty of the future, Scarlett delves into contemplation, preparing for what comes next.

Chapter 20

The New Beginning

Back in the tranquil atmosphere of Master Donovan's shop, Scarlett resonates with a different silence, as if the watches were awaiting the next chapter of the temporal story. The once-silent watches now seem to pulsate with renewed energy. Scarlett moves among them, each one representing crucial moments of her journey through time. Every tick-tock tells the tale of her epic temporal odyssey, from challenges in the Middle Ages to debates in the Conclave of Watches. The room is filled with the reverberation of her choices, and the young watchmaker plunges into deep reflection on the weight of her role as the guardian of time. As her eyes traverse the watches, Scarlett feels a mix of satisfaction and melancholy, knowing that, although her journey has come to an end, the imprints left in the temporal web will endure in every future tick-tock.

Through temporal messages and special connections, Scarlett's companions share their reflections on the temporal journey.

The group's cohesion is reflected in their thoughts, revealing how shared experiences have transformed their individual perceptions and emotional bonds. Each apprentice, from initial skepticism to active participation in the final adjustment, has been shaped by Scarlett's influence and the challenges faced together. Their messages distill a blend of nostalgia and hope, with expressions of gratitude for being part of a unique temporal odyssey.

Although the future is uncertain, the connection between them transcends temporal barriers, and each word shared through time resonates with the echoes of a friendship forged in the very fabric of time. The apprentices' alliance, despite tensions and challenges, has left an indelible mark on the temporal narrative, becoming a testament to the strength of collaboration and friendship across eras.

Scarlett contemplates the modified events and how they impact temporal reality. Previous conflicts are resolved, and pending plots find their conclusion. Each adjustment in time has its echo, and Scarlett faces the ethical implications of her decisions, pondering the responsibility that comes with being the guardian of time. As she observes the changes in the temporal plot, she experiences a blend of emotions: from the satisfaction of having saved crucial moments to the emotional burden of sacrifices made. The relationships she has forged throughout her temporal odyssey take on new dimensions, and the connections between characters deepen with the added meaning of altered events.

This moment of reflection plunges her into an internal journey, where the complexities of her role as the guardian of time intertwine with her own personal experiences, shaping the unique amalgam of her identity in the vastness of the temporal continuum.

Scarlett's internal conflict persists as she contemplates her future. Questions about destiny, free will, and temporal responsibility come to a climax. What role does she want to play after navigating the temporal currents? Crucial decisions about her life and purpose loom on the horizon. Reflection in the quiet atmosphere of Maestro Donovan's shop becomes an introspective act.

The clocks, though silent, seem to be silent witnesses to her deepest thoughts. The emotional connections she has cultivated throughout her journey and the lessons learned from altered events intertwine at the crossroads of her destiny. Each tick-tock of the clocks seems to resonate with the decisions she will have to make and the possible ramifications in her own temporal story. In this moment of contemplation, Scarlett faces the transcendent task of deciding her next chapter in the vast fabric of time.

Scarlett makes final decisions that will define her destiny and the course of time. The resolution of this ultimate choice sets the tone for the new beginning that lies ahead, marking the end of her journey through the eras. The time-traveling odyssey has come to its conclusion, but Scarlett's legacy as the guardian of time endures. Master Donovan's shop, with its witnessing clocks, falls silent, but the promise of a fresh start lingers in the air. Although Scarlett's temporal odyssey has concluded, the possibilities of a new chapter in the vast tapestry of time persist. Every choice she has made, every adjustment to the clocks, has left its imprint on the temporal fabric. The emotional burden of bidding farewell to companions and facing ethical dilemmas has shaped her character and left scars on her heart. Now, in this definitive moment, Scarlett reflects on the consequences of her role as the guardian of time and the decisions that will shape her future.

The silence of the shop serves as the backdrop to the anticipation of a new beginning as Scarlett prepares to close this chapter and open the doors to the unknown that awaits beyond the veil of time. Every choice she has made, every clock adjustment, has left its mark on the temporal fabric. The emotional weight of bidding farewell to companions and facing ethical dilemmas has shaped her character and left scars on her heart. Now, in this definitive moment, Scarlett contemplates the

consequences of her role as the guardian of time and the decisions that will define her future. The silence of the shop sets the stage for the anticipation of a new beginning as Scarlett prepares to close this chapter and open the doors to the unknown that await beyond the veil of time. As she gazes at the silent clocks that bear witness to her journey, Scarlett reflects on the profound impact of her odyssey.

The room, once filled with the ticking symphony of temporal possibilities, now echoes with the weight of her responsibilities and the gravity of her choices. The transition from the familiar to the unknown becomes a poignant moment of introspection, marking not only the conclusion of a temporal saga but the genesis of a fresh narrative waiting to unfold in the vast expanse of time.